Using Apideas

How to set up and manage Apideas for mating honey bee queens

First published 2022

ABC Practical Reference Series

First published 2022

Copyright © 2022 Daniel Basterfield
Illustrations © 2022 Daniel Basterfield
Photos © 2022 Daniel Basterfield and Kenneth Basterfield

Daniel Basterfield has asserted his right under the Copyright, Designs and Patents Act, 1988, to be identified as the author of this work.

'APIDEA' is a registered trademark of APIDEA Vertriebs AG, Switzerland.

All rights reserved. No part of this publication may be reproduced or transmitted in any form or by any means, electronic or mechanical, including photocopying, recording, or any information storage or retrieval system, without prior permission in writing from the author.

No responsibility for loss caused to any individual or organisation acting on or refraining from action as a result of the material in this publication can be accepted by the publisher or by the author.

A catalogue record for this book is available from the British Library.

ISBN (Hardback edition) 978-1-7391790-0-7
ISBN (Softback edition) 978-1-7391790-1-4

Building skills and confidence
Making the transition from novice to competent beekeeper
Opening horizons and de-mystifying the craft of beekeeping
Encouraging and developing 'thinking beekeepers'

Advanced Beekeeping Courses was formed in 2019 by Ken and Dan Basterfield, in order to provide practical tuition and guidance at a level suitable for experienced beekeepers.

Courses run at their purpose-built honey farm in Devon, UK, where they have a teaching apiary, classroom, and laboratory - in addition to a popular tea room with honey shop, pollinator gardens and wildflower meadows.

Advanced Beekeeping Courses
Blackbury Honey Farm
Southleigh, Colyton
Devon, EX24 6JF

www.advancedbeekeeping.org.uk

Contents

1 **Introduction** 2
    1.1   Photographs 9
    1.2   Measurements 9

2 **Getting ready** 12
    2.1   Three phases 12
    2.2   The queen raising pipeline 15
            2.2.1   Planning work around ripe queen cells 17
            2.2.2   Caging ripe queen cells for flexibility 21
    2.3   Assembling the hive parts 25
    2.4   Assembling and waxing frames 29
            2.4.1   Queen cells and frame orientation 32
    2.5   Entrance slider 36
    2.6   Feeders and feed 39
    2.7   Carrying mini-nucs 45
    2.8   Stands and tables 47
    2.9   A mini-nuc toolkit 51
    2.10   Filling cup 54
    2.11   Record keeping 56
            2.11.1 Written records 58
            2.11.2 Numbering mini-nucs 60
            2.11.3 Visual markers and push pins 62

3 **Establishment** 66
    3.1   Pre-flight checks 68
    3.2   Filling with bees 71
            3.2.1   Collecting workers 72
            3.2.2   Distribution of workers into mini-nucs 75
            3.2.3   Turning mini-nucs the right way up 78
            3.2.4   More selective collection of workers 79

	3.3	Queen cell introduction	81
		3.3.1 Candling queen cells	82
	3.4	Storing in the dark	84
	3.5	Putting Apideas out at dusk	87
	3.6	Checking for queen emergence	89

4 Management 92

	4.1	Timing of inspections	92
	4.2	Inspecting Apideas	94
		4.2.1 Lifting propolised frames	97
	4.3	Feeding	100
	4.4	Handling queens	103
		4.4.1 Picking a queen out of an Apidea	107
		4.4.2 Queen introduction cages	110
		4.4.3 Caging queens with workers	111
		4.4.4 Holding caged queens for short periods	115
		4.4.5 Queen re-introduction	117
	4.5	Recycle or close down?	119

5 Recycling 122

	5.1	Approach	123
		5.1.1 Queenless periods	123
		5.1.2 Broodright vs. queenright	123
		5.1.3 Emergency queen cells	125
	5.2	Managing population size	127
		5.2.1 Brood balancing	127
		5.2.2 Bolstering by exchange	128
		5.2.3 Bolstering with adult bees	129
		5.2.4 Bolstering with emerging brood	130

6 Closing down 132

	6.1	Equipment and preparation	133
	6.2	The unite	135
	6.3	Follow-up	135

7 Reading Apideas 142
- 7.1 Good population size 144
- 7.2 Population too small 146
- 7.3 Failed queen cell emergence 148
- 7.4 Entrance activity 150
- 7.5 Good combs 152
- 7.6 Erratic first laying 154
- 7.7 Constrained laying pattern 156
- 7.8 Laying workers 158
- 7.9 Queens with deformed wing virus (DWV) 160
- 7.10 Disease 162
- 7.11 Starvation 164

8 Advanced techniques 166
- 8.1 3-frame to 5-frame 166
- 8.2 Second brood box 171
- 8.3 Upper feeder 174
- 8.4 Entrance queen includer 175
- 8.5 Drawing Apidea combs in full-size colonies 176
  - 8.5.1 Frames of empty drawn comb 178
  - 8.5.2 Frames of brood 179
  - 8.5.3 Frames of stores 181
- 8.6 Over-wintering Apideas 182
- 8.7 Temperature monitoring 184

9 Disease and pests 188
- 9.1 Hygiene 188
- 9.2 Dealing with disease 189
- 9.3 Varroa 190
- 9.4 Chalkbrood 191
- 9.5 Nosema 191
- 9.6 Wasps 192
- 9.7 Badgers 197
- 9.8 Mice 199
- 9.9 Wax moth 201

		9.10	Woodpeckers	203

10 Maintenance 206

- 10.1 Cleaning Apideas 207
- 10.2 Repairs 212
  - 10.2.1 Frame repairs 212
  - 10.2.2 Polystyrene repairs 213
  - 10.2.3 Clear plastic repairs 214
  - 10.2.4 Red plastic repairs 215
- 10.3 Painting 216
  - 10.3.1 Paint colours 216
- 10.4 Spare parts 219
- 10.5 Storage 220

11 Clones & imitators 222

- 11.1 Earlier and later pattern Apideas 224
- 11.2 Rütli or MiniApi 226
- 11.3 Api'Deus Holz 228
- 11.4 Swienty Swi-Bine 230
- 11.5 The white copy 232
- 11.6 The green copy 234
- 11.7 Mini BiVo 236

12 Resources 238

- 12.1 Simple grafting calculator 239
- 12.2 In/out cards 240
- 12.3 Apidea inspection record sheets 241
  - 12.3.1 Using the record sheets 242
- 12.4 Establishment checklists 243

13 Closing thoughts 246

Index 248

1

1 Introduction

This book is aimed at anyone who would like to use Apidea mini mating nucs to produce a number of mated queens. Whether you are thinking of ten or a hundred Apideas, the principles and practices covered here will scale up accordingly.

Queen raising is one of the most interesting and rewarding aspects of beekeeping: it allows us to propagate the desirable characteristics of our best colonies throughout our apiaries.

Raising queens in any quantity more than 'a handful' can usefully be viewed as a pipeline, with distinct stages arranged according to the queen honey bee's developmental timetable. This pipeline could be envisaged in broad terms as:

Select → Raise → Mate → Introduce

The Apidea mating nuc caters for just one stage in this pipeline: **Mate** – the adoption of a ripe (i.e. soon-to-emerge) queen cell, and the care of that young queen once she has emerged. She will spend the first 2-3 weeks of her adult life in this Apidea until she comes into lay, whereupon she is moved onwards by the beekeeper to head up a larger colony.

The Apidea is not a general-purpose nucleus hive (nuc), nor is it suited to prolonged queen holding, or indeed overwintering. Rather it is designed for a single job: queen mating. Whilst any viable honey bee colony can be used as a mating hive provided that it is queenless, the Apidea is a purpose-designed miniature mating nuc that requires only a cupful of bees to stock.

To make even a dozen traditional mating nuclei requires a lot of donor colony resources: several thousand bees and a number of drawn combs full of brood and stores. The economy of using just a cupful of bees instead for each Apidea quickly becomes apparent. A strong colony might only spare sufficient combs and bees to make up two traditional 3-5 frame mating nucs, yet it could easily donate enough bees to stock a dozen Apideas with little apparent impact.

The details of the rest of the queen raising pipeline vary considerably based upon scale, method, and equipment used. As far as Apideas are concerned, ripe queen cells will have come from somewhere, and mated queens will have to be be moved on to somewhere else. Each stage needs to have the capacity to cope with the output of the previous stage (grafted larvae, queen cells, mated queens) when they need to be moved on.

Our only major consideration to enable the use of the Apidea is that the queen cell cup or carrier used at the **select** and **raise** stages allows queen cells to be moved safely and without fuss into the Apidea. This is discussed in more detail shortly.

In considering mating nucs of any size or format, we cannot overlook the developmental timetable inherent in queen raising: a queen honey bee takes around 16 days from egg laying to adult emergence. The presence of a new young queen is a catalyst for great change within a colony. Whether we view that change as desirable or not, it will happen according to a fixed biological timetable as soon as queen raising has started within a colony, regardless of the beekeeper's intentions, availability, forgetfulness, work commitments, or social calendar.

The Apidea mating mini-nuc is well known but comes without instructions. Despite its popularity, advice on using an Apidea is not always easy to come by, and can be variable in quality and relevance to the British climate.

Perhaps the most useful resource to date has been Ron Brown's slim booklet *Managing Mininucs – Honeymoon Flats for Honeybee Queens*, but in most queen raising texts the management of mini mating nucs may only account for a

1 Introduction

page or two - if it is mentioned at all. My purpose with this new book is to provide a good single reference for using the Apidea in particular, and mini-nucs in general.

Much has already been written about the various methods and systems of producing queen cells from selected colonies – and I will not attempt to duplicate this here. I would encourage the reader to invest in a copy of David Woodward's *Queen Bee: Biology, Rearing, and Breeding*, an excellent general practical text.

My father and I run up to sixty Apideas at any given time in our queen raising activities at our honey farm in Devon. My father was a founding member of the *Devon Apicultural Research Group* (DARG), and obtained his first Apideas in the mid-1980's. In those early years, DARG was a practical, experimental group - I remember well my father's experiments with various types of mini and micro mating hives, the frustrations with heat-retention issues with timber and Perspex even in the mild climate of South Devon, and the renewed interest when some brand new

Mating in Miniature

BIBBA produced a number of publications throughout the 1970's promoting the use of small mating hives made from wood and perspex.

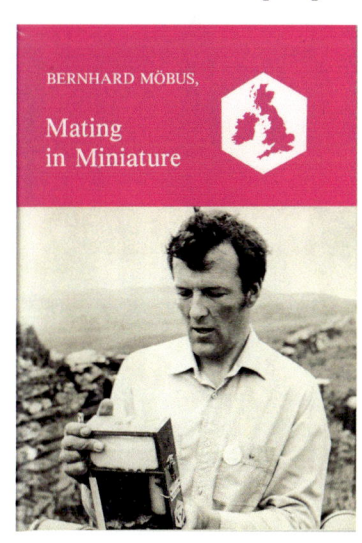

4

Using Apideas

Wooden mating nucs

Made by my father to a typical design of the late 1970's and shown here being trialled on our garage roof.

small orange-brown polystyrene boxes arrived and proved themselves to be much more successful.

We still have two of these first-generation Apideas, which were in use until very recently. They differ only in minor details from the current model, but in terms of function and materials they are essentially the same. Due to the interchangeability of parts and the annual strip-down for thorough cleaning, all the parts of these originals had become mixed with the newer ones. I kept noticing older-pattern parts in use, and gathered them together during the end-of-season clean-up in 2015. I thus retired them (in good working order!) after 30 years or so of service and keep them now as reminders of how well that first batch of Apideas served us.

During the recent fashion for beekeeping in new shapes and forms, various pieces of equipment came to the market that were generally over-styled and under-tested,

1 Introduction

Old vs new Apideas

On the left is the original form of Apidea, one of our first that I retired after decades of service. All parts are interchangeable with the later, more common pattern shown, but it is clear that a number of detail improvements were incorporated after the first few years of production.

with appealing designs, materials, and colours failing to mask significant flaws or compromises. It amuses me to think that the Apidea was decades ahead of its time as a polystyrene top bar hive.

By contrast with these more recent fashionable designs, much of the appeal of the Apidea is that it was carefully designed to meet a specific need, using (then) unconventional but logical materials to produce an elegant, durable, and workable design. Often, beekeeping equipment feels like it has been designed down to a price rather than up to a standard, for which penny-pinching beekeepers firmly bear the blame.

The Kirchain type of polystyrene mating nucs (also known as Kieler or Warnholz) devised in the 1960's and 1970's always feel just slightly too compromised to me in their design and function. The Apidea, on the other hand, is so 'right' that it has remained in use in essentially the same

Using Apideas

Absolute minimum?

John Atkinson's backpack contains 36 of his 'micronucs' on the way to Lundy Island, site of his isolated mating apiary experiments, to demonstrate just how small and portable a successful queen mating nuc could be.

form for over forty years. The Apidea is something of a unicorn: good, cheap, *and* durable all at the same time.

Such has been the success of the original that it has spawned many clones and imitators. Most are inferior, trading a trivial up-front cost saving for long-term frustration. I will use the terms **Apidea**, **mini mating nuc**, and **mini-nuc** interchangeably, however where there are specific detail differences between the Apidea and the various similar mini mating nucs, I will refer to the genuine Apidea as the standard. For example, I will always expect a clear crown board with a circular hole to accept a queen cell, or the plastic frames to have a top bar and two side bars, which are both features of the Apidea that are lacking in some of the imitators.

At so many points in this book I've been tempted to add the phrase "ask me how I know" to underline a piece of advice with a sense of self-deprecating humour. The simple truth is that we worked it out as we went along, and have learnt by making most of the mistakes imaginable. The point of writing it all down is to help you short-cut that learning process and avoid some of the frustrations. Thus what I present here is not the only way of doing things – that mythical *One True Way* which too many beekeepers mistakenly fixate upon – but it is what has evolved as our working practice during forty years of running many Apideas at a time.

My father initiated and managed the National Diploma in Beekeeping (NDB) programme of Short Courses, funded by the DEFRA *Healthy Bees Plan* from 2009-2019. We co-wrote the Queen Raising short course, and we presented this together for the ten year duration of the *Healthy Bees Plan*. Since 2019, we have continued to offer this two-day course (and the others we wrote and delivered for the NDB, progressively updated) under our own *Advanced Beekeeping Courses* umbrella. From the outset, the Queen Raising course has concentrated on raising by grafting and mating with Apideas, as being two areas where it is difficult to find good practical tuition at a local beekeeping association level. We have thus spent well over a decade teaching beekeepers how to use Apideas, refining how we describe and practice the various techniques we use, and fielding the questions that arise.

Much of my affection for the Apidea stems from the fact that that I greatly enjoy queen raising. Stocking the first Apideas of each season with bees and queen cells is a most welcome milestone in the beekeeping cycle, and a satisfying act of optimism. Of course every season works out differently, sometimes better, sometimes worse, but we beekeepers are nothing if not optimists.

I hope this book helps you to enjoy working with Apideas as much as I do.

1.1 Photographs

The photographs used here were often captured in the heat of the moment in the apiary with a smartphone pulled out of a bee suit pocket. Such photos were accumulated over several years during the writing of an article that grew into a booklet that grew into a book. Not all of the photos are of professional quality, but each has been chosen as it illustrates a pertinent or interesting aspect just as it was seen in the apiary.

They do say that the best camera you can own is neither the most expensive, nor the most technically proficient, but the one that is always with you.

1.2 Measurements

As a child of the 1970's, I was schooled in the then-novel metric system. However, growing up in a beekeeping family, it soon became clear that honey bees work in imperial measurements. Thus I adopted a natural hybrid system of units which allows anyone under the age of fifty to understand beekeeping measurements:

Millimetres up to **inches**
Inches up to **metres**
Metres up to **miles**

I will adhere to this system in the text to avoid confusion

1 Introduction

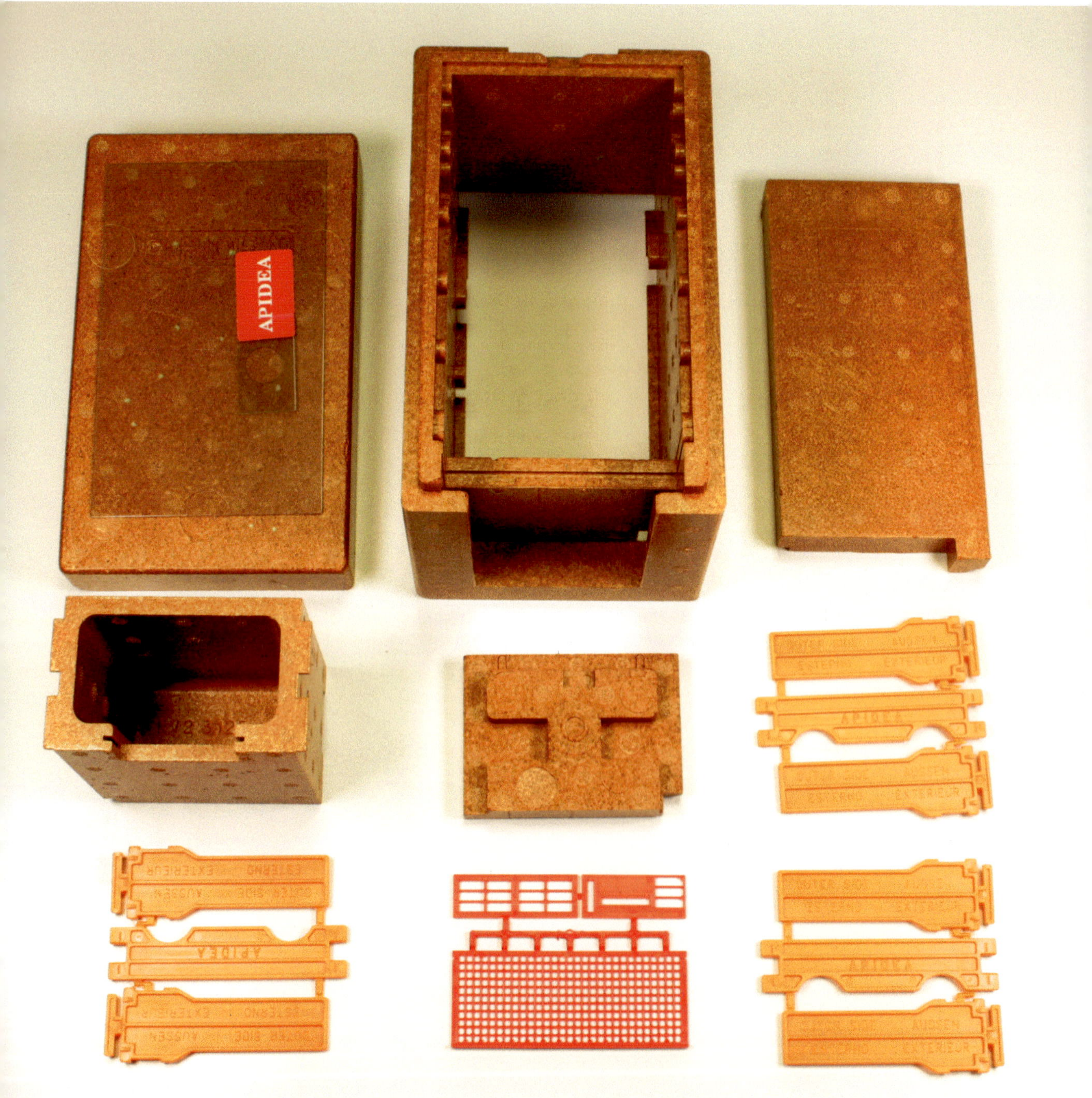
APIDEA

2 Getting ready

Queen raising runs on inflexible timelines determined by honey bee biology. Some planning, and a little preparation in advance - such as erecting tables for your Apideas to stand on, and readying tools, feed, and record-keeping sheets - will ensure that things run much more smoothly later on.

2.1 Three phases

Many beekeepers are taught or advised to consider an Apidea 'finished with' once a single queen has been mated. *"Set it up with bees, feed, and a queen cell; leave for three weeks, then check for a laying queen"* is typical advice. Whilst this does often work, it's really just scraping at the surface of what you can do with a mini-nuc. In fact, each mini-nuc you establish could mate three or four queens successively during that season.

I view the process of setting up and running Apideas as having three distinct but overlapping phases - **establishment**, **management**, and **recycling** - and consider an Apidea to only be fully ready for use once it has mated its first queen and it contains her brood. What others consider the end point is, for us, just the start! The flow chart overleaf summarises these phases and their relationship to each other. It gives an outline of the key tasks, checks, and decisions that underpin the transitions between these phases.

For **establishment**, the objective is to populate the Apidea with bees and an almost emerging queen cell. They need to achieve cohesion in their new home. Successful establishment comes when the queen has emerged, and creates a colony that closely resembles a small cast swarm, setting up home whilst its young queen takes her mating flights.

Once an Apidea has been successfully established, it needs ongoing **management** as a small queen mating colony that may not be sustainable without intervention. This is a subset of normal colony management, tailored to the specific purpose and vulnerabilities of a mini-nuc.

Using Apideas

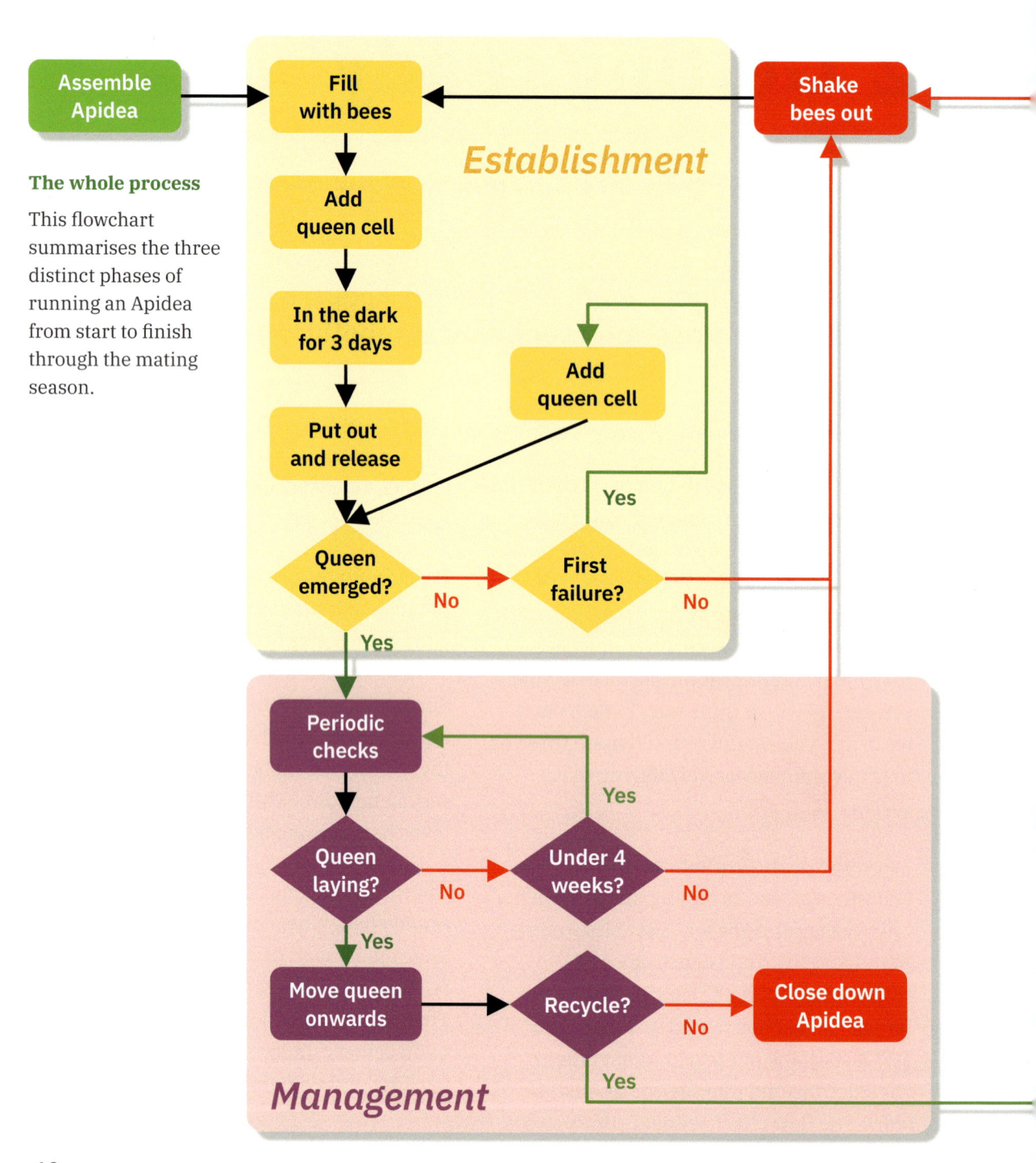

The whole process

This flowchart summarises the three distinct phases of running an Apidea from start to finish through the mating season.

Establishment

- Assemble Apidea → Fill with bees
- Fill with bees → Add queen cell
- Add queen cell → In the dark for 3 days
- In the dark for 3 days → Put out and release
- Put out and release → Queen emerged?
- Queen emerged? No → First failure?
  - First failure? Yes → Add queen cell (loop back)
  - First failure? No → Shake bees out → Fill with bees
- Queen emerged? Yes → Periodic checks

Management

- Periodic checks → Queen laying?
- Queen laying? No → Under 4 weeks?
  - Under 4 weeks? Yes → Periodic checks
  - Under 4 weeks? No → Shake bees out
- Queen laying? Yes → Move queen onwards → Recycle?
  - Recycle? No → Close down Apidea
  - Recycle? Yes → (back to establishment)

13

2 Getting ready

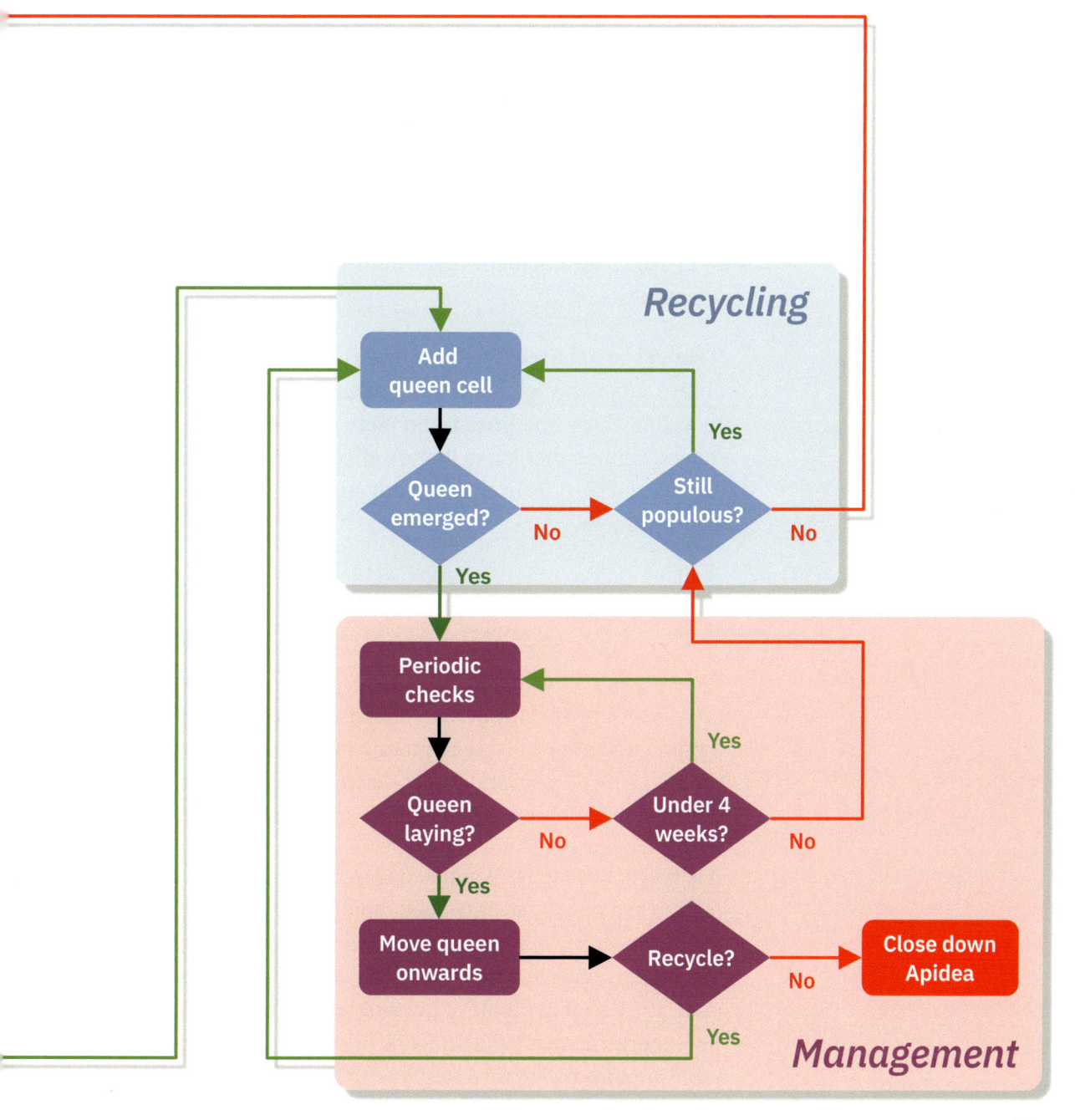

Recycling

- Add queen cell
- Queen emerged?
  - No → Still populous?
    - Yes → Add queen cell
    - No
  - Yes → Periodic checks

Management

- Periodic checks
- Queen laying?
  - No → Under 4 weeks?
    - Yes → Periodic checks
    - No → Still populous?
  - Yes → Move queen onwards → Recycle?
    - Yes → Add queen cell
    - No → Close down Apidea

14

After the first successful queen mating, an Apidea colony is a much more cohesive and sustainable entity. Combs will have been drawn out, stores and brood are present, and young bees will soon be emerging to replace the ageing and dwindling original workers. In this state, the Apidea is ideal for **recycling**: move the newly mated queen onwards, and replace her with another ripe queen cell from a queen raising colony. The process of queen emergence, mating, and laying can then repeat, and this is where the true efficiency of the mini-nuc becomes apparent.

It should be apparent from the flow chart that it is not always a one-way journey from establishment through to recycling; there are times when there are set-backs, or indeed failures that make it more effective to empty an Apidea and start from scratch with another attempt at establishment.

2.2   The queen raising pipeline

Whether you think of yourself as a large-scale or small-scale queen raiser, any activity that uses separate colonies for queen raising and queen mating follows a progression through several practical stages, each feeding into the next at a time determined by honey bee development.

It is impractical to hold mated queens for any great length of time in a mini-nuc since they rapidly run out of laying space. Queens will become frustrated and go off lay, and the workers will become frustrated with their non-laying queen and start to nibble at her and treat her roughly. It is my experience that laying queens that have been held in mini-nucs for two to three weeks can have tattered wings and paint removed by this treatment; shortly after this time you may find that your mini-nuc is either queenless or that its entire population has absconded.

One important aspect is that the capacity of your cell raising, queen mating, and queen destination stages must be matched, regardless of the scale of your queen raising. There is no point grafting 24 cells successfully if you only have six mating nucs available, nor having 18 mated queens in mini-nucs if you only have 6 queenless nucs to move them onward to. It is for this reason that I strongly advocate a 'little and often' approach to queen raising: plan on small numbers repeated as successive batches – it keeps the bottlenecks more manageable. Thus if your target is 24 mated queens, plan on producing four batches of six mated queens. Key to this planning is the fact that Apideas established in late spring can be reused for successive cycles of queen cell introduction, emergence, and mating through the summer.

There is one caveat, however: even when done well, queen raising is a process that suffers inherent losses at each step. Selected cells (e.g. grafts) may not be accepted, queen cells started may be abandoned before sealing, sealed cells may not emerge, queens may be lost on mating flights, and queen introduction is not always successful. When gaining experience of queen raising it is realistic to aim for a 50% success rate end-to-end: thus in the example just cited, to produce four batches of six mated queens, plan for at least four batches of 12 grafted larvae to allow for those cumulative losses.

With practice the success rate rises at each individual stage, but do not expect perfection. For example, our queen raisers run on Modified Commercial frames, and

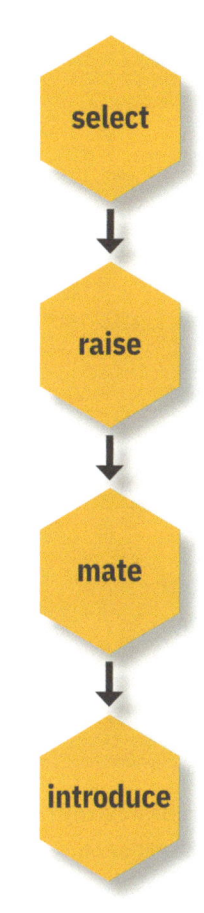

Queen-raising pipeline

Any activity that uses separate queen raising and mating colonies follows a progression through several practical stages, each feeding into the next at a time determined by honey bee biology.

Using Apideas

each cell bar holds 13 grafts, which naturally becomes my 'little and often' grafting batch size. I consider the acceptance and raising of ten or more grafts per cell bar to be a success.

2.2.1 Planning work around ripe queen cells

When raising queens, one of the most significant and fixed timescales is that of the 12 days from cell starting to queen emergence – i.e. day 4 through to day 16, with egg laying on day 1. Unfortunately this immediately prevents you from scheduling queen raising tasks around a weekly or fortnightly cycle.

The reason that this is a fixed timescale is that not only will raised queens begin to emerge to this timescale, but that the emergence of a young queen into a queen raising colony initiates the swift destruction of the remaining queen cells. All that work is lost. Furthermore, unless that slender and flighty young queen can be quickly found and removed, this colony can be written off for any successive batches of cell raising.

Do remember that the development times from egg laying to emergence commonly quoted of queen 16 days / worker 21 days / drone 24 days are averages. Read carefully the

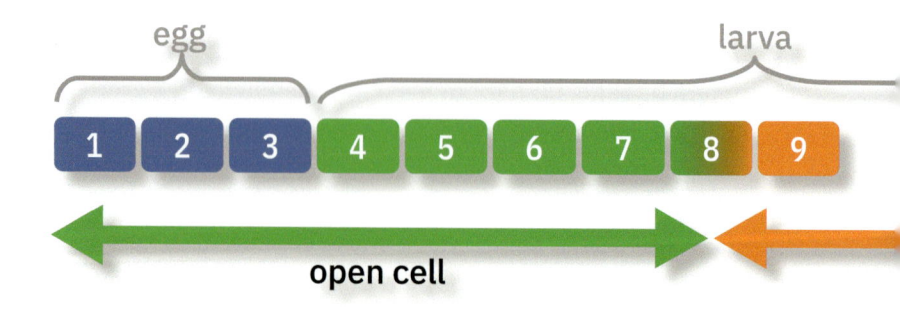

Queen cells destroyed after queen emergence

This is what happens when you mis-record your grafting dates or mis-calculate your moving on days. A queen has emerged and, aided by the workers, the remaining ripe queen cells have been destroyed. Worse, there's now a virgin queen on the loose somewhere in your queen raising colony…

Changes in the developing queen

Adapted from Ted Hooper's table Days from Laying of Egg in Guide to Bees and Honey, showing only the visible changes in the developing queen between cell sealing and emergence. These physical changes can provide very useful indicators if you open one of a batch of queen cells in order to verify the stage of development, especially when the exact dates of egg laying or cell sealing are unknown.

Developmental change	Day
Cell sealed	8
Spinning cocoon	9
Fifth moult to pupa	10
Eyes pale red	
Eyes red	12
Eyes purple, thorax yellow	13
Abdomen yellow	14
Antennae darken	
Moult of pupa to adult	15
Emerges from cell	16

likes of Mark Winston's The Biology of the Honey Bee and you will see that he notes that queens have been observed to emerge on day 14-17 from egg laying, with the variability ascribed to both genetic factors such as sub-species differences, and environmental factors such as brood nest temperature and nutrition. Also note that even for the accepted average, queens do not emerge "after 16 days", but "during day 16" – the two are not the same. I refer to almost-emerging queen cells – ones at day 14 or 15 – as **ripe queen cells**.

Development timeline

If your queen raising is to be successful, you need to be completely familiar with the timings of the developmental stages of the queen, and also understand that the oft-quoted absolutes are actually averages. Sealing and emergence are two critical stages that take place at inexact times, usually during days 8 and 16 respectively.

Using Apideas

It is because of this variability that I work with a safety margin, and aim to move ripe queen cells out of queen raising colonies and into mating nucs on day 14, i.e. ten days after grafting (which should have been done with larvae in their 4th day). If I grafted a little on the large side, day 15 might be pushing my luck, and day 16 would definitely be living dangerously!

The act of "moving on of ripe queen cells" sounds straightforward – after all, they're only a handful of acorns – however it is the readying of their destination where the time-consuming work can lie. This is especially true when you are making up Apideas for their first use (populating with bees and so on) or indeed making up more traditional queenless nucs to receive those queen cells.

Thus when planning my grafting, I start not by identifying suitable days for grafting, but suitable days for moving on the resulting ripe queen cells, including any work of setting up or otherwise preparing their recipient mating nucs. Having identified a moving day, I count ten days back to find grafting day. Who said beekeeping doesn't take over your life?!

To assist in the general logistics, I have developed two aids. The first is that I write explicit grafting records with

Expect some failures

Success isn't automatic in queen raising. Even when things go well, there may be small losses at each stage. Take these in your stride.

Here, for example, the earlier grafts (on the upper cell bar) show an acceptance rate of 10 out of 13 cells - actually a good acceptance rate.

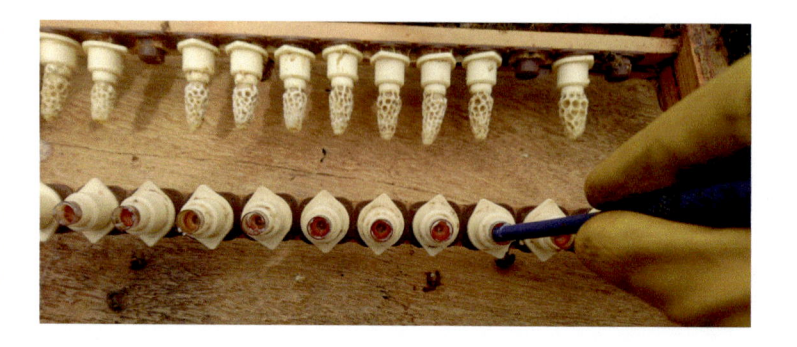

Visible grafting records

Chalked on a bookcase in my office, these records are seen at least twice a day. The crucial date is 'out', when queen cells need to be moved on. 2012 was a poor beekeeping season, with prolonged cool and wet spells. Note that three initial cycles of grafting resulted in poor acceptances (out of 13 grafts to a batch), then after a fortnight of trying it all came good. Persevere!

chalk pen on the glass bookshelf doors in my office – I look at this at least twice a day, so they're hard to miss. It could just as easily be a dedicated whiteboard, of course. The second aid is a simple slide-rule type of reckoner that I made up for double-checking corresponding grafting and moving days.

The grafting records are written up immediately after performing a graft, and the recipient colony, date, and number of grafts are recorded. Calculated forward from the grafting date are the anticipated dates for moving, mating, and egg laying, based upon the following simple timings:

10 days after grafting is 'moving day' - move the ripe queen cells onwards to mating nucs;

14 days after moving day - queens should be well into mating;

> **21 days after moving day** - mated queens are likely to have begun egg laying.

By explicitly recording the planned moving date for each graft, I can see at a glance which moving days are coming due, and how much work is associated with each. This I find far less error-prone than just recording grafting days and having to work out the subsequent dates on-the-fly.

When grafting colonies are revisited – e.g. to check acceptance, or perform a subsequent graft – brief notes are taken and then the number for any previous graft is adjusted on the bookshelf to reflect the actual count of accepted & sealed cells that will eventually need to be moved on.

Once a batch of grafts has been moved on, I lightly cross through the whole row to retain the record but clearly indicate that the critical task of moving the queen cells on has been completed.

2.2.2 Caging ripe queen cells for flexibility

I have experimented with caging queen cells in queen raising colonies prior to emergence. It is very easy with the Jenter style cell carriers, as you can buy plastic 'hair roller cages' to slip over them. In my experience it only works reliably if you can cage on day 14 and release on day 15 or 16, and thus provides a short delay useful in two scenarios:

> **You can't spare the time** on day 14 to make up additional mating nucs, but could do this on day 15 or 16;

You 'grafted a little large' back at the outset and probably used 36-48 hour-old larvae, meaning that some may indeed emerge early on day 15.

If you do this, remember to add a little fondant or honey in the indents in the bottom cap of the cage – this will provide a ready food source even if the young queen is ignored by the workers outside.

With normal access to queen cells, workers thin down the wax around the cell tips very shortly before emergence – on days 14 and 15 – and this greatly aids queen emergence. There is a temptation with caging to extend the caged period a day or two either side of this 14-15-16 window, and this is where I have found it to be unreliable, with queens trapped in cells that remain heavily waxed at the tips.

I much prefer the far simpler solution which is to choose your grafting days not by when it feels like a good day for grafting, but by identifying an available 'moving day' in your schedule and counting back ten days to pinpoint the corresponding grafting day. That way you plan your grafting around your availability on the most critical day of the queen raising process, rather than grafting and then having to juggle your schedule around moving day.

Chapter 12 - *Resources* - presents a simple grafting schedule slide rule that you can download and print out. This was designed to very quickly calculate grafting days from move onward days, and vice versa.

2.2.3   When to add queen cells

When dealing with an established mating nuc, adding a queen cell is straightforward, as per normal management (colony queenless, no emergency queen cells). However when setting up a mating nuc for the first time, there are two differing schools of thought as to when the queen cell should be added:

> **Add queen cell as soon as the mating nuc has been made up, before storing in the dark.**
>
> **Add queen cell after the colony has been stored in the dark and then put out.**

I favour the first approach – queen cell added immediately – since the mating nuc then contains more elements of a cohesive colony from the outset.

If the queen cell is viable, the workers will attend to it and begin drawing comb during the 3 days of confinement, and will be evenly distributed across the back two frames and the feeder. On the other hand, after 3 days either without a queen cell or with a non-viable queen cell, the workers will be clustering in the feeder and are unlikely to have started drawing comb. This difference in worker distribution is immediately apparent through the clear crownboard.

The queen will emerge whilst the Apidea is in the dark for the requisite three days. Whilst she is initially of little interest to the workers, as her glands (and thus her attractiveness) begin to develop the young queen becomes an accepted element of the little colony during this period of confinement.

Once an Apidea has been put out and the workers are able to fly freely, significant differences may be seen between the two approaches when the queen cell should be added. An Apidea with a recently-emerged queen is much more likely to retain its workers, whilst workers from a queenless Apidea are much more likely to drift and disperse away.

The approach you prefer will determine whether you establish Apideas at the point that the first ripe queen cells become available, or three or four days before this deadline. In describing the establishment of Apideas in detail in the next chapter, I assume that you are adopting the 'queen cell added immediately' approach, as I do.

Using Apideas

2.3 Assembling the hive parts

The Apidea comprises five polystyrene parts: floor, hive body, entrance slider, feeder, roof. Where these slide together, the parts are keyed such that it is difficult to assemble them incorrectly. The feeder sits at the back of the hive body, the floor slots in from the rear, and the entrance slider has a notch in one corner that should be aligned with the corner entrance in the hive body.

The roof is the only part not keyed to indicate its preferred orientation, but should be placed with the 'APIDEA' text legible when facing the front of the hive. This aligns the circular cut-outs in the underside of the roof with the hole in the crownboard to allow plenty of clearance for any

Complete Apidea parts

Polystyrene:
1. Floor
2. Hive body
3. Feeder
4. Entrance slider
5. Roof

Clear plastic
6. Crownboard

Red plastic
7. Feeder queen excluder
8. Entrance queen excluder
9. Ventilation grille

Orange plastic
10. Frame top bar & side bars

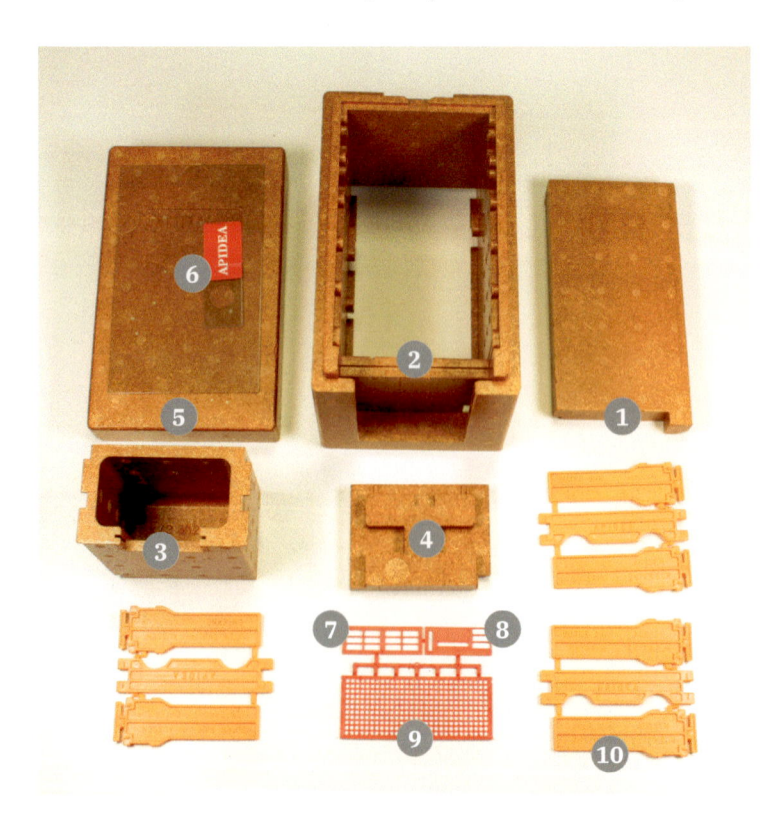

2 Getting ready

Frame parts

1. Top bar, upper
2. Side bar, outer
3. Top bar, underside
4. Side bar, inside

form of queen cell carrier. Placing the roof the other way round, these cut-outs do not align and a queen cell might be obstructed or dislodged, leading to failure to emerge.

A bundle of smaller red and orange plastic parts is provided within, variously moulded together with little sprue parts to cut off and discard, much like an Airfix model.

The three orange frame pieces are obvious – each piece comprising two side bars and a top bar moulded together. Twist off the surplus sprue parts, and the side bars twist and click into place on the ends of the top bar.

Frame top bars

The upper surface is indented and has 'APIDEA' moulded in the centre.

The underside has a pair of parallel ridges for locating foundation. The semi-circular cut-outs are to aid queen cell placement.

Using Apideas

Frame assembly

Visualise how foundation might be fixed between the parallel guides on the inside of the top bar and side bars.

The frame on the **left** is incorrect: both the top bar and side bars are the wrong way round.

The frame on the **right** is assembled correctly. All the writing is on the outside!

The grooves on the underside of the top bar, and at the inner tops of the side bars, are intended to act as guides for inserting and securing foundation. As you will see later, it is not necessary to give complete sheets of foundation.

The large red grille sits across the front upper opening in the hive body, slotting into grooves there, with a hooked

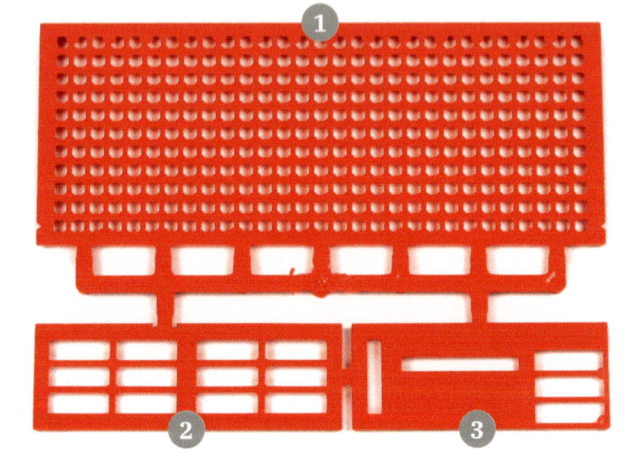

Red plastic parts

1. Ventilation grille
2. Feeder queen excluder
3. Entrance queen includer

edge intended to point backwards to retain the front edge of the crownboard.

The purpose of the two smaller red grilles is less obvious at first. One, with equal-sized slats acts as a queen excluder for the feeder, slotting into grooves either side of the moulded access aperture on the feeder's front. The other is an optional queen **in**cluder for the entrance, to allow queens to be selectively contained within an Apidea.

The clear plastic crownboard has a circular hole covered by a hinged flap which should be on the upper surface and to the right of the hive when viewed from the front.

There is a notch at the upper rear of the hive body which allows you to get a finger under the rear edge of the crownboard to lift it; the hooked edge on the large red grille prevents the crownboard from sliding forwards, so instead it pivots upwards. Just one of those nice details!

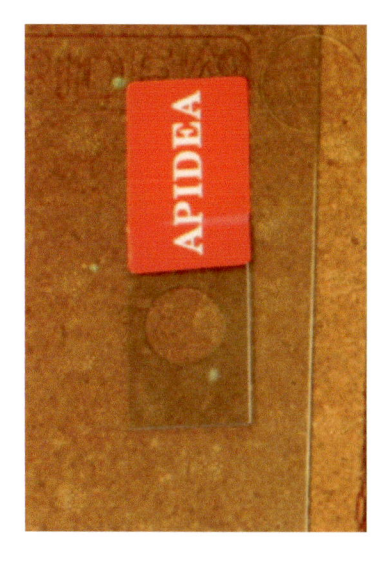

Crownboard: flap covering hole

An 'APIDEA' sticker acts as a hinge for the flap. The hole beneath it is just the right size to support the 'cork' of a Jenter or Nicot queen cell carrier.

2.4 Assembling and waxing frames

The Apidea frames come in three parts – two side bars and a top bar. Bundles of spare frames can be bought cheaply and are a useful investment for spares or for running 5-frame Apideas. Have a few more to hand than you think you might need!

There is no bee space between the outside of the side bars and the inside of the Apidea wall. Unless your bees are very prone to propolising, this will not cause problems within use, particularly if your Apideas are run seasonally rather than year-round. (Langstroth and Dzierzon can rest easy on this occasion.)

The side bars are clearly marked with 'Outer side' (in four languages) to indicate the outer side. If you assemble them the wrong way round, the resulting frame will not fit easily into the Apidea because the triangular comb supports make it too wide. The top bar has a pronounced groove on

Frame waxing equipment

A double saucepan on a small electric hob allows for a convenient source of molten wax. The drinking straws will be used to pick up and dispense molten wax. Have everything laid out ready before you start.

its underside, intended to guide the placement of wax starter strips. I use pieces of damaged foundation cut into roughly 1" x 2" rectangles as these starter strips.

Any surplus pieces of unwired foundation can be quickly sliced into starter strips using a straight edge and a pizza cutter.

To attach the starter strips, use a double pan arrangement to melt a small amount of beeswax. It doesn't need to be perfectly clean, just reasonable recycled wax that you would not be embarrassed to exchange for foundation at a trade show. You need a pool of molten wax about an inch deep.

Position a frame, inverted, so that you can easily offer a starter strip up to the groove on the underside of the top bar. Have that starter strip close to hand.

Take a paper or plastic drinking straw, and submerge the end in the molten wax. Cover the upper end of the straw

Cutting starter strips

With a frame top or bottom bar held as a straight edge, use a pizza cutter to slice roughly 1.5" x 1" pieces of unwired foundation as starter strips.

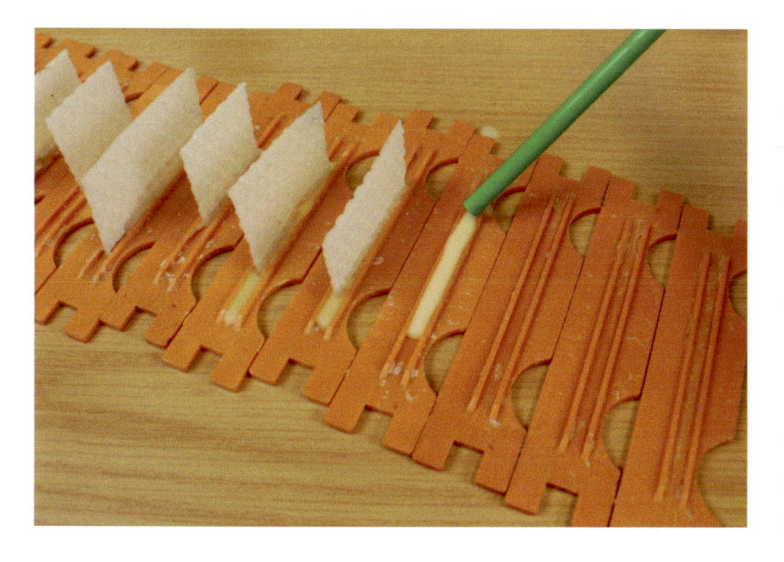

The wax bead

With small movements of your thumb over the top of the straw, you can control the flow of wax to dispense a nice bead just where you want to attach a starter strip.

(This wax bead has cooled too much to insert a starter strip, but shows up so much better for the camera than the amber molten wax!)

30

Using Apideas

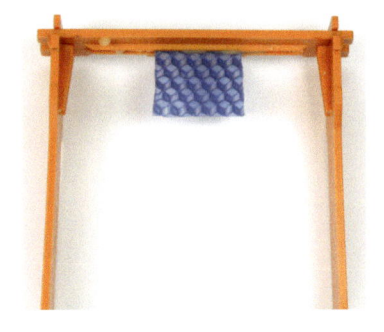

Coloured foundation dispersal

Using coloured wax for starter strips demonstrates just how much wax is recycled from foundation sheets during comb building, and how far it is dispersed.

with your thumb, then lift the straw. As long as your thumb forms an airtight seal at the top of the straw, the wax cannot run out. For the next 5-10 seconds your straw becomes a liquid wax dispenser – lift your thumb to allow the wax to flow, lower your thumb to stop the flow. Play with the straw over the wax pan to get a feel for the start and stop motions. Return the straw to the wax pan between uses to prevent it from becoming blocked by solidifying wax.

Assuming you're right-handed, pick up a starter strip with your left hand and hold it ready, close to the top bar. With your right hand, fill the straw and then, run a bead of molten wax along the top bar groove. Before the wax can cool, insert the edge of the starter strip into the waxed groove, and hold the strip vertical. Within seconds the wax turns opaque as it cools and you can let go of the starter strip now - it should be secure.

If you wobble the starter strip whilst the wax 'glue' is setting, or feel that you needed more wax than you originally put in the groove, you can use a second application of wax to provide extra adhesion. Neatness of the wax bead is not crucial since the bees will of course recycle any excess when comb building.

With practice, this becomes a very quick and accurate process. By laying out frames and starter strips beforehand, you can quickly wax up a whole batch of frames for many Apideas within minutes.

If you have spare sheets of candlemaking wax – essentially coloured unwired foundation – then you can use these for starter strips. It is an interesting experiment to use coloured wax to see how far it permeates the resulting combs – it is clear that bees pare down the foundation when forming the midrib of drawn comb, recycling that excess wax in cell building. Using coloured foundation in an observation hive exhibits the same result on a larger scale and creates an interesting talking point.

2.4.1   Queen cells and frame orientation

It is important that you make a conscious decision as to how the frame top bars should be orientated, rather than just filling boxes with frames. You do not want to realise that your frames are wrongly arranged when you have already put the bees in but cannot get your queen cell in!

This frame orientation choice will depend upon the type of queen cell cup that you will be using. The two crucial frames are the second and third back from the entrance – under the circular hole in the clear crownboard, where the queen cell will be inserted.

The top bars have a semi-circular cut-out on one side only. By changing the orientation of the frames, we can make three different presentations of the top bars below the crown board hole, as shown here.

Frame orientation	Suits cell carrier
Circular	Jenter & Cupkit
	JZBZ (with card support)
Semi-circular	JZBZ (without card support)
Parallel	*none*

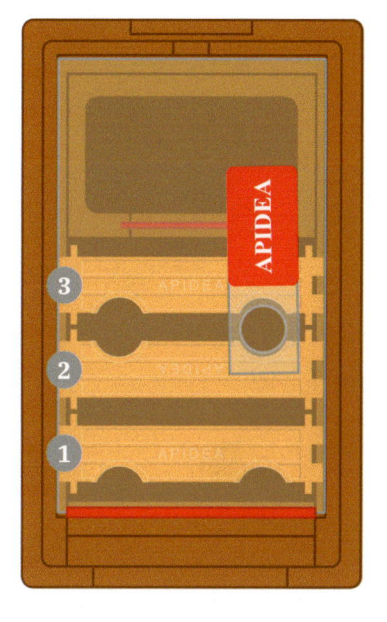

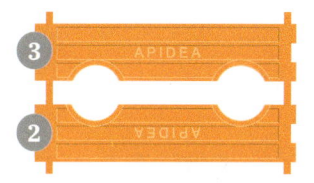

Circular

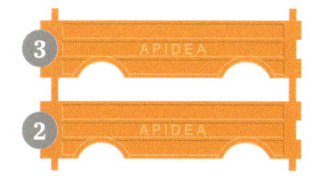

Semi-Circular

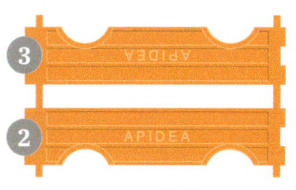

Parallel

Cell cups compared

From top to bottom:
- JZBZ
- Cupkit
- Jenter

The circular arrangement should be considered the standard as it is by far the most useful, especially if you are using a Jenter or Cupkit system, or grafting into their cell cups. With a simple adaptation, it also suits the JZBZ cups.

My preference when grafting is to use the cell cup & cork arrangement of the Nicot Cupkit system within cell bar frames, bypassing the use of the big plastic box of fake comb (into which the cell cups are intended to be first placed). The cell cups, corks, and cork holders of this system are cheap and readily available in quantity as spare parts without buying the whole kit.

The Nicot Cupkit is, as far as I can see, a continuation of the original Jenter system; both have an identical simple translucent plastic cup that fits snugly into a plastic cork. Parts sold for a 'Corpularva' system appear to be identical to the Cupkit ones, and inevitably there are many anonymous copies available on eBay and the like.

The current Jenter system is a second generation design, and much more fiddly that the original: the translucent cup is made of two parts (base, walls) that fit together and then slot as a unit into the plastic cork. Frankly, if you have the eyesight and dexterity for manipulating these small parts in the apiary, then grafting is probably preferable as being quicker and cheaper!

The circular hole in the Apidea crownboard is perfectly sized for the plastic corks common to all these systems, holding it securely. Indeed the circular indents in the underside of the roof are there to give clearance to this arrangement. It is highly likely that the Apidea was intentionally designed to accept the components of the

Card square for JZBZ cup

An inch square of light card supports a JZBZ cell cup over the open crownboard hole of an Apidea. Punch a 1mm hole through the card, and it will comfortably grip the 2mm spigot on a JZBZ.

early Jenter system, or vice versa, since these were concurrent queen raising innovations.

The otherwise simple and functional JZBZ cell cup is frustrating to insert into an Apidea because its flanged part is slightly too small to hold it over the crownboard hole in the way described above. Squeezing a JZBZ in between a semi-circular top bar arrangement feels like a bodge. It does fit and hold, but it's prone to lifting the crown board and feels only-just-secure, so is vulnerable to popping the cell through onto the floor of the Apidea with any rough handling or jolts. If a queen cell drops to the floor, there is a high risk of failure to emerge.

For JZBZ cups, I have had success using roughly 1" squares of cereal box card with a 1mm hole punched through the centres of them using a fine-pointed biro. These fit securely over the 2mm spigot of the JZBZ, allowing it to be suspended cleanly through the hole in the crownboard with a circular top bar arrangement. I half expected the cardboard to turn to mush and the JZBZs to drop through, but they work reliably.

Natural queen cells cut from the comb cannot readily be suspended through the flap in the crownboard, and thus

Slipped JZBZ

This JZBZ cup had been wedged between frame top bars but had slipped. Fortunately this was in an Apidea being recycled, which already had drawn comb that caught and held the queen cell. Had the cell have dropped to the floor, this queen probably wouldn't have emerged.

Using Apideas

pose a problem. This includes queen cells raised directly on the comb (such as those from the Miller method) or queen cells raised on wax cups directly attached to a wooden bar (such as the Alley 'strip' method). Such cells would ordinarily be cut with a generous 'heel' of wax that would allow them to be pressed securely into the comb of a queenless colony. This does not work at the initial mini-nuc establishment stage - not only will you lose just-introduced bees opening the mini-nuc to insert the natural queen cell, but more importantly there is generally only foundation present at this point, so no comb for the queen cell to adhere to.

If the wax surrounding a natural queen cell can be carefully trimmed away with a sharp knife, that cell can usually be suspended by first placing it in one of the double-pronged press-in queen cell cages, and then dangling this arrangement through the crownboard hole. Frames would need to be in a circular arrangement.

Regardless of whichever queen cell carrier you use, if the frames have been incorrectly orientated then this is far easier to remedy whilst the Apidea is empty than when it contains somewhat agitated newly-introduced workers whose over-riding instinct may be to depart at any opportunity. Making a conscious decision at the preparation stage and having a dry run with your preferred queen cell carrier will avoid frustrations later. Like all things, though, it is mainly by getting it wrong and losing the workers whilst fumbling to turn frames around that you fully appreciate the frame orientation question!

Natural queen cell suspended using cell protector

Carefully trim away surplus wax from around the queen cell, so that it can be slid into one of these double-pronged cell protectors. Suspend the cell and protector through the crownboard hole.

Note that the flap should never be allowed to close over a suspended queen cell of any sort.

35

2.5 Entrance slider

The entrance slider fits at the front of the hive body, and controls both ventilation through the red grille, and access through the small entrance hole in the hive body.

The entrance slider should be slid into the front of the hive body. The slider can be lifted or lowered to selectively open or close the entrance, and when the entrance is open it can be moved further upwards to adjust the amount of ventilation available.

The notch on the entrance slider should be on the lower right, as viewed from the front, matching the position of the entrance hole in the hive body. This notch probably reduces the likelihood of the slider crushing or guillotining inquisitive bees poking their heads out from within the hive body as the entrance is closed.

When new, the entrance slider moves stiffly, and holds firmly in any position. With use, however, the slider quickly becomes slack and will drop - causing an unwanted (and potentially catastrophic) sealing of the entrance. Wedging a small stone under the open slider is an obvious way of preventing unwanted closing, but such a stone is often lost when the Apidea is lifted or moved, and clearly doesn't help keep a slack entrance slider closed when we are inverting well-used Apideas to fill them.

A push-pin pressed into the polystyrene of the entrance plinth acts as a good stop for the slider, being just over bee space in height. Importantly, the pin will stay in place when the Apidea is lifted and tilted - in fact they usually stay put even if an Apidea tumbles off a table. For filling,

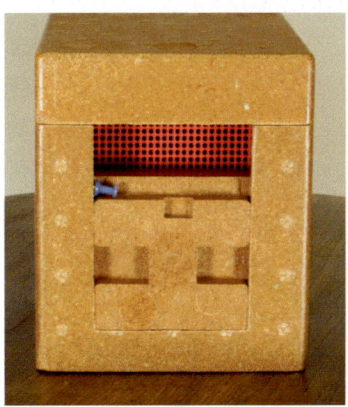

Entrance slider secured with a push pin

Push pins allow for the entrance slider to be positively secured, either in the open position (upper photo) or closed position (lower photo). This becomes important when the entrance slider loosens with age and wear.

the pin position is changed so that it prevents the slider from opening.

The downside of using pins is that the entrance area of your Apidea can become something of a pin cushion. However, with a little care you can easily re-insert a push pin into an existing pinhole, avoiding a proliferation of pinholes over time.

As you will see when I discuss record keeping, I use coloured push pins as markers to indicate the status of each Apidea. I always carry a box of these pins as part of my Apidea toolkit, so always have spares to hand for securing entrance sliders either open or closed.

A notable side-effect of using a push pin to keep the entrance slider open is that good ventilation is provided through the red grille at all times. About two thirds of the grille area is exposed. It is uncommon to see significant propolisation across the grille perforations - an indication that the bees are not troubled by this degree of ventilation; they would surely restrict the grille with propolis if they were.

There seems to be a common received wisdom that Apideas should be placed in dappled shade to avoid absconding due to overheating in the midday sun, but we can't recall ever experiencing this here in south Devon, including in the most recent mini-heatwave of 2022. I do wonder if our use of push pins ensures ample ventilation at all times, and whether cases of absconding may have arisen in Apideas where the slider has been left fully raised, thus covering the ventilation grille?

By curious coincidence, a classic 4x2 Lego brick slots in

perfectly as a support for an open entrance slider, although it is not as securely located as a push pin, all too readily falling out when the Apidea is handled.

Several of the Apidea copies use markedly different entrance arrangements, some even incorporating a disc-type entrance cover to allow various permutations of open, closed, and ventilated to be dialled in. These copies are discussed in Chapter 11 - *Clones and Imitators*.

Entrance slider supported by a Lego brick

A classic 4x2 Lego brick slots in quite snugly under the left hand side of the slider. It almost seems designed for the task, until you tip or invert the Apidea, whereupon it readily falls out.

Using Apideas

2.6 Feeders and feed

Apideas have three feeder options. Every Apidea comes as standard with a removable feeder which occupies frame positions 4 & 5 (from the entrance). You can also purchase a larger feeder which fits over the Apidea body, in essence a mini Ashforth feeder. In practice there is a third option, that of adding frames of sealed stores taken from another Apidea. Assuming that everyone starts from scratch, I will concentrate on the standard removable feeder, referred to from now on as simply **the feeder**. The pros and cons of the optional top feeder are discussed in Chapter 8, *Advanced Techniques*.

Do not be tempted to use liquid feed in the feeder. Bees will drown unless you arrange a float or ladder, and topping-up with sugar syrup risks starting robbing of these vulnerable little colonies. There is, however, a far more significant reason for not using liquid feed: you need to have the feeder filled before you introduce the first bees to a fresh Apidea, and to introduce those bees you must turn the Apidea upside down and fill through the sliding floor. Solid feed is therefore a must.

The removable nature of this feeder suggests that in practice we would swap out empty feeders for filled ones in one deft manoeuvre. Great in theory, however as soon as the feeder is lifted by more than a bee space, inquisitive workers rush under to investigate the new-found space. Slotting in another feeder – or indeed replacing an accidentally lifted feeder – would crush these workers. Attempting to shoo the inquisitive workers from under the removed feeder is a futile activity akin to herding cats. If you have made this mistake, the only easy solution is to slide out the Apidea floor entirely, re-insert the feeder,

Apidea feeder options

From top to bottom:

Standard feeder

Optional Apidea feeder

Frame of honey

then carefully slide the floor back in place – which is an even more perilous and frustrating task. Thus the Apidea has a removable feeder that, for all intents and purposes, cannot be routinely removed and replaced.

Adding fondant or candy directly into the feeder works well, until you need to top it up. At this point you have some remnants of old feed, probably quite dry, and bees who are unwilling to vacate the feeder however much you smoke or cajole them from above. Dropping more feed in on top risks entombing those bees. Fortunately, white plastic 8oz cut comb containers will slot straight in to the feeder aperture. Filled with baker's fondant, cut comb containers become **feed cartridges**. Thus the removable Apidea feeder stays put, no bees are crushed, yet we can safely and easily remove empty containers and exchange them for containers of fresh feed.

Baker's fondant is not fully solid and will slowly flow at hive temperatures. If a container of fondant without a lid were to be slotted into the feeder, the fondant would slump

Feed cartridge made using a cut comb container

Cut comb containers fit perfectly in the Apidea feeder, and allow fresh fondant to be added (or dried old fondant to be removed) with ease. Here the empty container is being removed and a full container stands just behind the Apidea, ready for exchange. We refer to these as 'feed cartridges'.

Using Apideas

Cut comb container lid cut for access

By cutting roughly a finger's width of one end of the clear plastic lid, we arrange for easy bee access. Ensure the gap is placed upwards!

and stick to the feeder walls, rendering it very awkward to remove the container until the fondant had been completely consumed. To restrain the fondant but provide access for the bees, cut a clear cut comb container lid so that it can be left in place but still provide bee access. The simple route is to cut a finger's width off one end of the lid, a more elegant route is to use a leather punch to make a circular hole in the lid. Whichever you choose, ensure that you have removed the tab which projects from one corner of the clear lid – if left in place this will cause the container to sit just high enough that the Apidea crownboard will not fit comfortably over it.

You might be wondering, after all of this, why the feeder is removable and not just moulded in, as in some of the Apidea copies? It's so that the feeder can be replaced by two extra frames during favourable conditions; alternatively, if you are adding a second brood box, the feeder can be moved out of the lower (original) box and slotted into the same location in the new upper box.

Running on 5 frames or with a second brood box are described in Chapter 8, *Advanced Techniques*.

A standard 12.5Kg box of baker's fondant cuts up to fill about 40-44 cut comb containers. If you fill the cut comb containers to the moulded line, they will contain 300g of fondant but in use the lids will stick to the fondant in transit, particularly if the containers are stacked on each other. When the lids are exchanged for cut lids, you then have lots of sticky spare lids to deal with. Far easier to fill the containers to just below the moulded line, with approximately 285g of fondant, and not have the sticky lid situation in the apiary.

Chill the fondant beforehand to make it stiff, or it will rapidly slump and spread as you cut it. Simply leave it overnight in a cool place. Open the box, lift out the bagged fondant, invert the bagged fondant over a kitchen cutting board and peel away the bag. Use a 3" or 4" wallpaper scraper to slice through the fondant, cutting blocks of roughly the right size to fill a cut comb container. Place

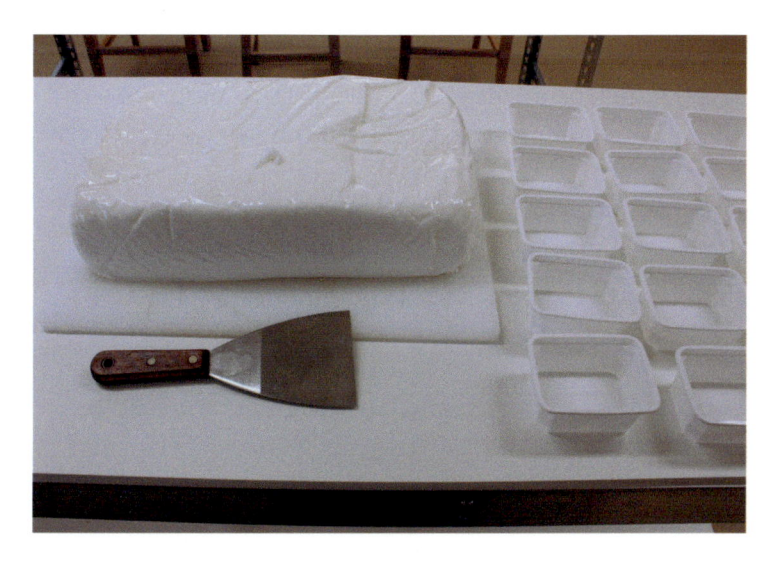

12.5Kg block of fondant ready for cutting

Fondant block on cutting board with wallpaper scraper for cutting and cut comb containers laid out ready for filling.

Using Apideas

Slicing fondant with a wallpaper scraper

Wallpaper scraper being used to cut fondant into smaller blocks that are then pressed into the cut comb containers.

A stock of fondant cartridges

Uncut lids are fitted to keep the fondant moist until needed. By taping the box flaps, the fondant box can be used to carry its former contents once divided into feed cartridges, making them very easy to manage in the apiary.

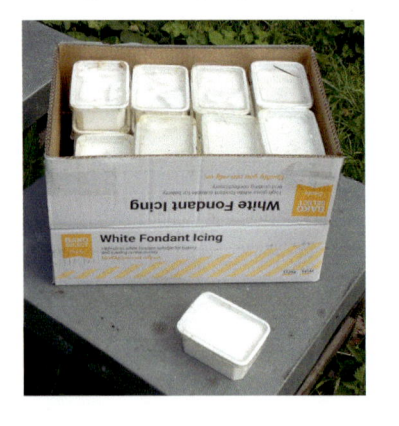

uncut lids on the filled containers so the fondant stays moist and soft until required – if stored in a cool place out of direct sunlight, the fondant will stay moist for a month or so. You can thus take a stock of pre-filled feed cartridges with you when inspecting Apideas, and rapidly change out old cartridges for new, swapping the existing cut lids across.

Bakers' wholesale suppliers sell 12.5 Kg boxes of fondant to the trade, but are generally unwilling to supply in small quantities. Either source fondant through your local baker, or consider registering your local association for a trade account. Either way, you will find that this fondant is a fraction of the cost of the formulated bee feed fondants sold through the beekeeping equipment suppliers.

Ensure that you only use basic 'Baker's fondant', containing sugar, water, and glucose syrup. Avoid any flavoured or coloured fondants, due to possible harmful effects of the added ingredients, and do not mistake ready-to-use cake icing sold in supermarkets for fondant. Confusingly, the bakers' suppliers often refer to their basic fondant as "fondant icing". Check the ingredients list to be sure of what you are getting!

Incidentally, we use larger plastic tubs – as typically used by Chinese takeaways - to carry emergency fondant feed for nucs or larger colonies. It's the same principle as Apidea cartridges, but scaled up. These translucent lidded containers are available cheaply in boxes of 50 or 100 online or from the more general wholesalers such as Booker and Makro in the UK; even the shallower tubs hold around 600g of fondant.

Just like the Apidea feed cartridges, a supply of these can be made up in advance and will stay moist whilst the lids are securely in place. If a colony needs an emergency feed then the lid can be removed and the tub inverted over the feed hole of the crownboard, where it sits comfortably in the void under the roof. Do not quite cover the feed hole - leave a beespace gap for ventilation and to allow bees trapped in the roof space to exit. Since the whole container is transparent, it's even easier to assess whether the colony is using the fondant and when the container should be replaced.

Fondant cartridges for full-size colonies

The same idea applied to full-size colonies: a quick feed boost when needed. Just as easy to transport without stickiness, and easy to see how much has been consumed.

Using Apideas

2.7 Carrying mini-nucs

With practice, four or six mini-nucs can be easily and securely carried by hand, but only if stacked two across and one, two, or three rows high. It is tempting to try to carry rows of three by holding the outermost two and squeezing them together, but any lapse in concentration or stumble at dusk turns this into a recipe for disaster: the lower middle roof remains fixed but the whole body of the lower middle mini-nuc falls away, spilling its contents over your feet.

A national or commercial crown board makes an excellent tray for six Apideas. These can be strapped and secured with hive or ratchet straps to carry them securely by hand or in a wheelbarrow or vehicle.

Alternatively, garden centres sell green 'tray tidy' items which fit six Apideas nicely and also double-up as general beekeeping stickiness limiters, e.g. under supers stacked in the car or in the kitchen awaiting extraction.

Carry Apideas by hand in two stacks not three!

Two stacks of Apideas can be comfortably and securely carried by hand. Do not be tempted to carry three stacks, since with the slightest wobble the lower middle Apidea will drop to the floor, spilling its contents.

Crownboards and straps

A crown board just holds six Apideas; by sandwiching and strapping as shown, Apideas can be carried securely.

45

When carrying populated mini-nucs in a vehicle, do not be tempted to stack them since they will move and tumble with the motions of the vehicle. Instead keep to a single layer across the floor of the vehicle, spaced to allow adequate ventilation. Cut a suitably shaped piece of plywood for levelling the floor if necessary. Be cautious about pushing and pulling mini-nucs into and out of a vehicle, since any loose floors may slide out of position and the bees will quickly escape.

Whether carrying by hand, wheelbarrow, or vehicle, remember that your queen cells are only as secure as the cell cups holding them, and that even familiar tracks to apiaries may be surprisingly bumpy when carrying a fragile load. A queen cell that drops to the floor of the mini-nuc generally fails to emerge. If you have JZBZ's "sort-of wedged" between top bars then these may easily be dislodged, whereas the positive fit of the Jenter or Cupkit corks prevents dislodging.

Garden centre tray tidies

Trays sold in garden centres can be very useful for carrying supers or brood boxes in vehicles, catching drips and debris. They can also be ideal for carrying six Apideas securely.

Carrying Apideas in a vehicle

A sheet of plywood gives a broad flat bed in the back of this Land Rover. Do not stack Apideas on each other since they might tumble. Rows are spaced for good ventilation… until you need to stop suddenly! Facing the hives towards the rear door enables a quick at-a-glance check that all entrances remain closed.

Using Apideas

2.8 Stands and tables

Before you put your mini-nucs out to mate, arrange some sort of stand, bench, or table for them at a convenient and comfortable working height. As a bonus, it will keep them out of the reach of badgers, who will quickly learn to turn out the frames and devour the tasty contents if they encounter mini-nucs at (or close to) ground level.

Simple stands can be made from fence posts with a plywood platform mounted on top, of at least 10" x 12" to accommodate a pair of mini-nucs facing in opposite directions. These look smart but with two mini-nucs give no space to lay the roof, frames, and such like when you open up a mini-nuc to inspect it. They work well with one nuc but are inefficient if you have more than a handful of mini-nucs in use.

A bench arrangement – a plank supported by two or more posts – allows for much more flexibility. Leaving gaps between the mini-nucs on the bench allows for working space during inspections.

A platform on a post holds two mini-nucs

Initially appealing, but where do you put the parts of one Apidea whilst you inspect it?

A simple bench

Two posts supporting a broader, longer bench allows for much more flexibility during inspection than with a small platform on a single post. There is now space to move the brick aside, invert a roof, and begin to inspect an Apidea. Just avoid the temptation to pack too many in, and ensure that entrances are neither adjacent nor facing each other.

A much more useful table can be made quickly and cheaply with standard 1.2m x 1m pallets. If you have an abundance, simply stack up four or five pallets to give a useful table height.

If pallets are hard to come by or the ground is uneven, lay a single pallet on the ground, drive in four posts tight against the corners and then lift and screw the pallet at a convenient height, cutting off any excess length of post so that they are flush with the pallet top. An extra pair of hands helps greatly with this, as does a spirit level. Choose a pallet with solid timber corner blocks as these will last for several seasons. Pallets with chipboard corner blocks will deteriorate rapidly; the screws holding the legs will work loose - potentially tipping your Apideas onto the floor. In this way, you can make sturdy, level, Apidea tables with minimum materials, even on rough or sloping sites.

Large and small pallet tables

Standard 1.2m x 1m pallets make great tables for ten Apideas. Larger pallets (used for delivering sheet materials) have capacity for 16-18 Apideas. Here the large pallets are shown with legs driven into the ground and sawn off flush with the pallet top.

Using Apideas

When using a pallet table I like to place a pair of mini-nucs at each corner, arranged in an L shape facing outwards, plus a pair on a diagonal in the centre facing in opposite directions. This ensures that no two entrances are facing, yet allows for ten Apideas with good working space between, plus space for your toolkit and record sheets to be kept close to hand. A slightly tighter packing will get 12 Apideas onto the same pallet, but you lose much of the working space; in this arrangement it is difficult to place removed roofs and frames without them being in close to the entrance and flight path of an adjacent colony.

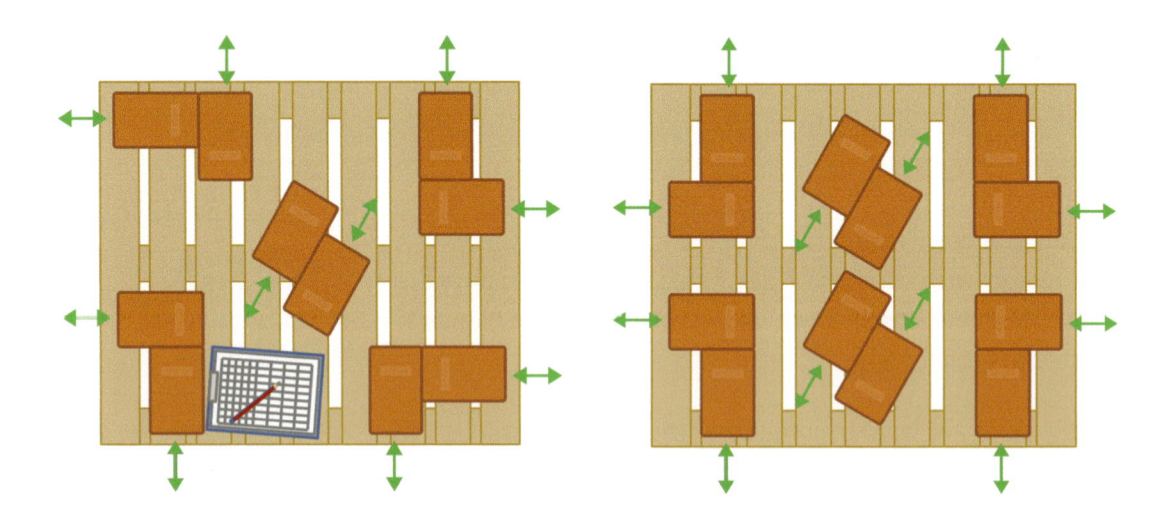

10 Apideas on a standard pallet table

Easy to orientate mini-nucs to avoid adjacent or facing entrances, and to ensure that either roof bricks or exposed frames are not put in the direct flight line of another colony during inspection. Good working space between mini-nucs, including space for notes, a clipping & marking kit, and a box of pins readily to hand.

12 Apideas on a standard pallet table

Easy to orientate mini-nucs to avoid adjacent or facing entrances. Much less free space to work during inspections, (where to put removed bricks, roofs, and frames?) or for necessary paraphernalia such as the notes, clipping and marking kit, and box of pins.

Ten Apideas arranged on a simple pallet table

This layout allows for good working space but keeps nearby entrances distinct and generally pointing in different directions.

The larger lightweight pallets used for some sheet building materials and glazing supplies are even better as table tops, accommodating 6-8 further Apideas, but need six legs to avoid sagging in the middle. Such improvised tables can be surprisingly durable – we have had them last for four years without paint or preservative.

Lightweight polystyrene mini-nucs can easily be blown off tables or stands. I therefore keep a supply of half bricks or fist-sized stones in mating apiaries. Alternatively, ratchet straps or bungee cords can be used to make tie-downs to secure Apideas to the tables and stands.

As with choosing an apiary site in general, avoid placing mating mini-nucs at excessively exposed or windy sites. Excessive wind chill will reduce perceived temperatures and discourage or delay mating flights; queens returning from mating flights may be blown off course.

2.9 A mini-nuc toolkit

Just as managing mini-nucs requires a subset of colony management skills, plus some extras specific to mini-nucs, so it is with your toolkit. Many items in your normal toolbox will be unnecessary, yet some extra tools help with mini-nuc tasks. Gather a dedicated toolkit so that you have all you need (and nothing you don't!) close to hand when working through your mini-nucs.

My toolkit consists of:

> **Clipping & marking kit**
> **Box of coloured push pins**
> **Clipboard with record sheets & pen**
> **Slender J-tool**
> **Smoker, fuel, lighter**
> **Fresh feed cartridges**
> **Filling cup**
> **Empty box or bucket**

We will look at the filling cup shortly. The last item – the empty container – is to retain discarded feed cartridges

Complete mini-nuc toolkit

The full toolkit taken to the mating apiary for Apidea inspections.

and lids, and removed queen cells. These are the natural and surprisingly prolific detritus of working with mini-nucs!

Keeping your record sheets on a clipboard holds them in order - add an extra bulldog clip to avoid page-turning by the slightest breeze. Clip or tie your pen onto the clipboard to avoid it rolling away and tumbling down through your stack-of-pallets table.

If your queen raising colonies are in the same apiary as the mini-nucs, you will also likely be carrying your grafting kit (tools, magnifiers, queen cell carriers, etc.) so that you can keep your 'little and often' grafting routine going.

Whilst working with Apideas you will occasionally need a hive tool for lifting propolised frames. Frames can generally be withdrawn easily with fingertips alone, but when they are stuck, they are stuck. I've detailed in section 4.3 - *Lifting propolised frames* - how I do this without damaging the polystyrene, using a carefully chosen slender J-tool.

Beware that not all J-tools are created equally. Most of the cheaper J-tools are clumsy at best, with the J-end either too long or too broad for Apidea inspection purposes.

The nicest hive tools are those made for many decades by tool and cutlery manufacturers Taylor's of Sheffield under their *Eye Witness* brand. These Eye Witness hive tools are truly the Rolls Royce of hive tools. Their J-tool is available direct from Taylor's as their 'Strong combination tool, no. 79/4', retailing at around the £10 mark. The slender J-end of these tools just slips perfectly between the frames of an

Tools kept close to hand when inspecting Apideas

Ideally there is space on the tables for the records, push-pin box, and clipping & marking kit, so these are immediately to hand as and when they are needed.

Using Apideas

J-tools compared

Top: Swienty's mini tool

Middle: Thorne's mini tool

Bottom: Taylor's standard J-tool, no. 79/4

Perhaps surprisingly, the mini hive tools were not well suited to the Apidea mini hive. The slender J-end of Taylor's 'Eye Witness' tool makes it ideal. Most other J-tools are too chunky for Apideas.

Apidea to lift them safely.

EH Thorne in the UK produce a £10 stainless steel J-tool (product code M5117) which is almost identical to the Taylor's pattern – certainly just as slender where needed on the J-end for mini-nuc frame manipulation.

I have tried a number of the 'mini tools' available from the equipment suppliers, on the very reasonable assumption that a mini tool should be ideal for a mini hive. Sadly I have not found this to be the case, even with Swienty's high quality little red hive tool. The various mini tools are all clumsier than a full size Taylor's J-tool, principally because their J-end readily slips into and through the comb under the top bars due to an odd angle and/or lack of a fulcrum notch. Swienty's tool is, however, very well made, like all their equipment, and does make a very fine beekeeper's bottle opener - Skål!

2.10 Filling cup

A carefully chosen filling cup allows you to stock each mini-nuc with the same measured and appropriate number of bees. Whilst on odd occasions we have improvised with honey jars or tin cans, a handled cup with a thin flattish rim makes both scooping and depositing bees far easier.

By chance an old melamine camping teacup seemed to be just right for this job, but having used that cup for nearly 20 years that particular style appears unavailable now.

Partly to avoid the risk of losing our one-and-only cup, and partly because there's no use teaching people to use an unavailable item, I looked around for an alternative. A one pint plastic milk bottle is ideally suited to the job. There are two sorts generally available: a tall thin one and a dumpy squat one. The tall thin bottle holds its shape better after cutting.

I measured our melamine cup by filling it with water, to find that it held 250ml to the brim. I then poured the same volume of water into the empty plastic milk bottle. Putting

Using the filling cup

The filling cup is used to scoop bees out of the collecting box and deposit them into the upturned Apidea during establishment.

Cups compared

The melamine camping cup and the cut-down milk bottle cup. Both have a volume of 250ml and should contain around 600 bees.

Measuring the milk bottle for cutting

Add 250g of water and invert, then mark the water level (dyed blue here) and cut to this line. These taller thinner milk bottles have useful notches up the side that help with marking and cutting straight!

the cap on tightly and standing it inverted, I marked the water level around the bottle and then cut to this line. This left the handle as part of the filling cup. In practice, I have found this milk bottle cup to be better than our old melamine cup, due to the very square edges, which allow for efficient and fuss-free filling with bees.

In recent years, the owners of the APIDEA brand have issued a flyer giving very brief instructions for the setting up of Apideas; they recommend 300 bees. I froze one of our melamine cupfuls, filled level to the brim as we do, to immobilise the bees for counting: just over 600 bees. I would not be happy in our climate establishing Apideas with just half the number of bees that we normally use.

You may be reassured to know that despite two hours in the deep freeze, all of the counted bees then thawed out in the sunshine and departed back to the donor colony. (This resilience can be a concern when dissecting bees; keep them in the deep freeze at least overnight to ensure they will not revive under the microscope.)

2.11 Record keeping

It is quite possible to run a number of mating mini-nucs without any form of records, but you will need to inspect them all at each visit to determine their status. With more than a handful of mini-nucs in operation this rapidly becomes impractical, so it is desirable to keep written records. If your mating apiary is remote then records are even more important since the mini-nucs cannot be casually checked for visual markers such as pins.

The records that we need to keep for mating nucs are very different to those for full-size colonies, or even for general purpose nucleus colonies. We do not bother to record temperament (irrelevant), stores or feeding (sufficient feed at all times is implicit in the management), disease (no disease signs should be tolerated – close down, remove, and clean any such mini-nucs), numbers of frames of brood or seams of bees (simply note if particularly strong or weak), and so on. Just as the mini mating nuc is a pared-down hive with a specific purpose, so too should be the record-keeping that accompanies it.

Thinking back to a mating nuc's place in the queen mating pipeline, the records must be able to answer at a glance two fundamental questions:

> **How many mating nucs are ready to accept queen cells?**

> **How many queens are mated, laying, and ready to move on?**

Whatever form they take, your mini-nuc records should readily answer these two questions, allowing a swift

Using Apideas

No.	QC date	QE	Eggs	Brood	Clip + mark	9/5 date	14/5 date	23/5 date	29/5	date	date
7	6/5	✓				QE	VQS		VQS weak		
13	6/5	✓	✓		✓	QE	VQS		C+M		
~~15~~	~~6/5~~	✗				QnE					

Record sheet example

Record sheets for mini-nucs are much simplified and should show you at a glance the progress with queen mating in each mini-nuc.

totting-up of the numbers ready for either task.

I will discuss in the next section some of the record systems I have evolved through. I have settled on a combination of written records and coloured pins. The written records are kept on printed tabulated sheets, and are useful for counting and planning, particularly with our remote mating apiary. The visual markers can speed up tasks in the apiary, but more importantly they work even when it is raining and you have to leave your clipboard under cover whilst you attend to your mini-nucs.

Record sheets in use

By a process of evolution, we now have a plastic clipboard, a bulldog clip to stop the wind lifting pages, waterproof paper, and a pressurised ballpoint (that writes in the wet) tied on with string. The record sheets are now almost impervious to rain, propolis, honey, or drips from the wash bucket!

2.11.1 Written records

Whilst I refer to these as 'written records', I do not differentiate between notes in a diary or on printed tabulated sheets, or a spreadsheet held on a tablet computer. The important thing is to have a usable record that works for you.

I have experimented with various formats of records over the years, and discuss these in Chapter 12, *Resources*. They are provided as downloads for you to compare and try out for yourself. There is no single perfect record sheet!

Each sheet records the progress through key mating steps for each mini-nuc, but varies in how or whether inspection notes are gathered, and how or whether key steps are dated. The key steps to record are:

1. **When was a queen cell given?**
2. **Has a queen emerged?**
3. **Are eggs present?**
4. **Is brood present?**
5. **Has the queen been clipped and marked?**
6. **Is the queen ready to move onward?**

I have returned to version 2; it has the simplicity of an at-a-glance checklist with space to record notes from up to five successive inspections.

Each numbered mini-nuc's records are only relevant during the current cycle of queen emergence and mating. Thus when a queen cell (or virgin) is added to a mini-nuc, any existing record line is crossed out on the sheet and a new record line is started to reflect the current cycle.

The main down-side of this approach is that as the season progresses the records become very jumbled, requiring much to-and-fro to find a specific mini-nuc's current record. With the v4 record sheet you can alleviate this by leaving 3-4 blank lines between each mini-nuc record when you start records at the beginning of the season, allowing successive cycles to be recorded below the earlier records for the same mini-nuc. Unfortunately this approach fails with the v2 sheet since the inspection date columns rapidly get out of sync, leading to confusion.

If you prefer to use a tablet in the apiary, a 'live' spreadsheet can be quickly sorted or filtered to show records of interest. To avoid unwanted stickiness, wrap the tablet in cling film - this can be replaced as needed and is a far more cost-effective approach than any of the rugged waterproof cases.

Number mini-nucs on all four sides aids location

Taking a few seconds more to number each face of a mini-nuc makes it so much easier to locate a specific one across the tables or stands in the mating apiary.

2.11.2 Numbering mini-nucs

The simplest form of numbering for mini-nucs is to use a large permanent black marker pen and write a number on each of the four sides of the main body. Having the number on all sides means that any desired mini-nuc can be located quickly and easily, regardless of their orientation or where you are in the apiary. It saves a lot of time otherwise spent walking round the tables. Unless you regularly survey your mating apiary from above, there is no value in numbering the roofs.

The marker pen numbering will need to be renewed once each season (and certainly after painting), which I do when the mini-nucs are checked and assembled prior to first usage. The pressure of the pen tip makes a slight impression on the polystyrene, meaning that over several seasons the number becomes gently embossed. The ink will still fade in prolonged bright sunlight, but a combination of four numbered sides and the embossing effect means it is hard to completely lose the number for any particular mini-nuc. Bullet tip markers give a more

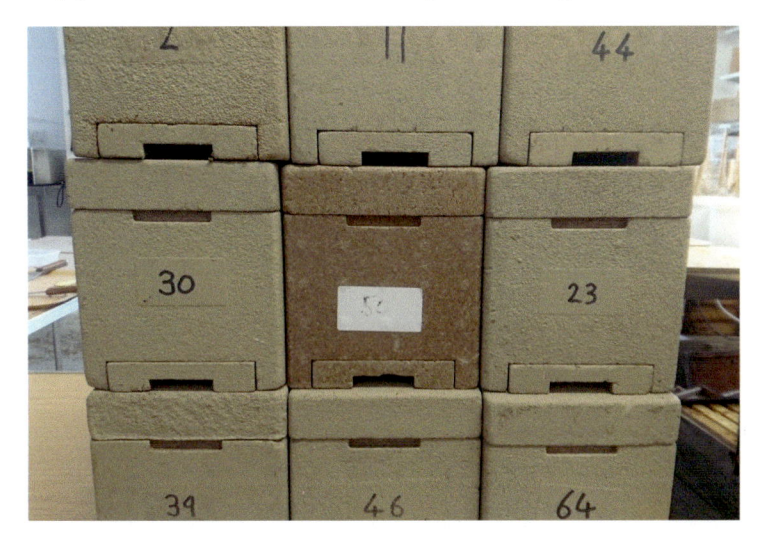

Unreadable number stickers

'Polylaser' stickers are durable, but both laser toner and permanent marker ink fade quickly from them. Write directly on the polystyrene or paint instead!

Using Apideas

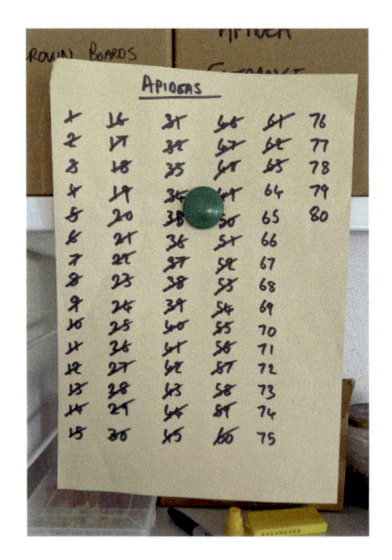

Number allocation sheet
If you are numbering mini-nucs as you use them, or after painting over existing marks, a simple number tracking sheet avoids the confusion of duplicate numbers.

pleasing script (and indent) than chisel tip, which have a tendency to dig in to the polystyrene.

I have also tried numbering via paper or more durable 'polylaser' label stickers, either hand-written by permanent marker or laser printed. Paper stickers are a waste of time, dissolving rapidly into mush. Whilst polylaser stickers are durable, laser toner does not withstand the elements and even permanent marker ink seems to fade rapidly on these stickers – either approach has a tendency to revert to crisp, white, unnumbered rectangles by the end of the season!

When numbering new (or re-painted) mini-nucs, ensure that you don't allocate the same number twice – any duplicates will be very frustrating. I once discovered that we had two number 55 Apideas in use; a quick stroke of the marker pen sorted this out, with Apideas 55 and 155 co-existing without any further confusion. Since we have about seventy Apideas, after re-painting them I keep a sheet of paper in the Apidea store with unallocated numbers written on it. Each time an Apidea needs a number, the next available one is chosen, written on the Apidea, and crossed out on the sheet. This is particularly helpful if you are numbering them as you put them into use.

2.11.3 Visual markers and push pins

Stones are great. A stone on the roof of a mini-nuc can signal any number of points of interest or imminent tasks. Perhaps it means that this one is ready for a queen cell, or that the queen within is clipped and marked?

In the short term, stones can be very useful to highlight mini-nucs requiring a specific task just before it is performed. For example, you might go round with the paper records and place a stone on any mini-nuc ready for a queen cell, then follow around with the queen cells themselves. It makes for less fiddling and therefore less risk of damage to those precious queen cells. However, the multi-purpose nature of the stone is also its downfall, despite its low cost and general abundance, both of which will continue to appeal strongly to your cost-conscious and inventive 'inner beekeeper'.

We have evolved a 'Red – Amber – Green' system of marker pins as visual indicators of Apidea status. A single pin is placed in the upper notch on the entrance slider, to indicate the following:

- 🔴 `Queenless; awaiting a queen cell`
- ⚪ `Queen cell added`
- 🟡 `Queen cell emerged or virgin introduced`
- 🟢 `Queen clipped and marked`
- 🔵 `Queenless; emergency queen cell present`

Pins at the entrance

The yellow pin indicates that the queen has emerged but is not yet laying.

We use blue pins for supporting the entrance slider as this is the least-used colour in our system.

Using Apideas

Push pin box

Small plastic compartmental clip-shut boxes - as sold in craft shops and fishing tackle shops - are very useful for keeping the push pins and small Apidea parts organised and to hand in the apiary.

The one pictured is a Bahco PTB402220; it is just right with six compartments and measuring roughly 9" x 5" when closed.

We use standard push pins (sometimes called map pins) with roughly 1cm high coloured plastic grip parts. They come in convenient assortment packs of four or five bold colours – usually our familiar queen-marking choices of white, yellow, red, green, and blue.

These pins are also useful in pinning loose entrance sliders closed, or providing a minimal beespace closure for an open slider. The colour of the pin used to support the entrance slider has no relevance to the state of the Apidea. We tend to use blue pins since they are the colour least frequently used in the above system, and so there is always plenty of them in the pin box.

If it wasn't for the need to apply a weight to the mini-nuc roof then I'd stick the marker pin in the roof so that it would be visible from any direction, just like the numbering. Perhaps the next evolution of the visual markers will be a quantity of half-bricks or large pebbles painted variously in the usual five colours…?

2 Getting ready

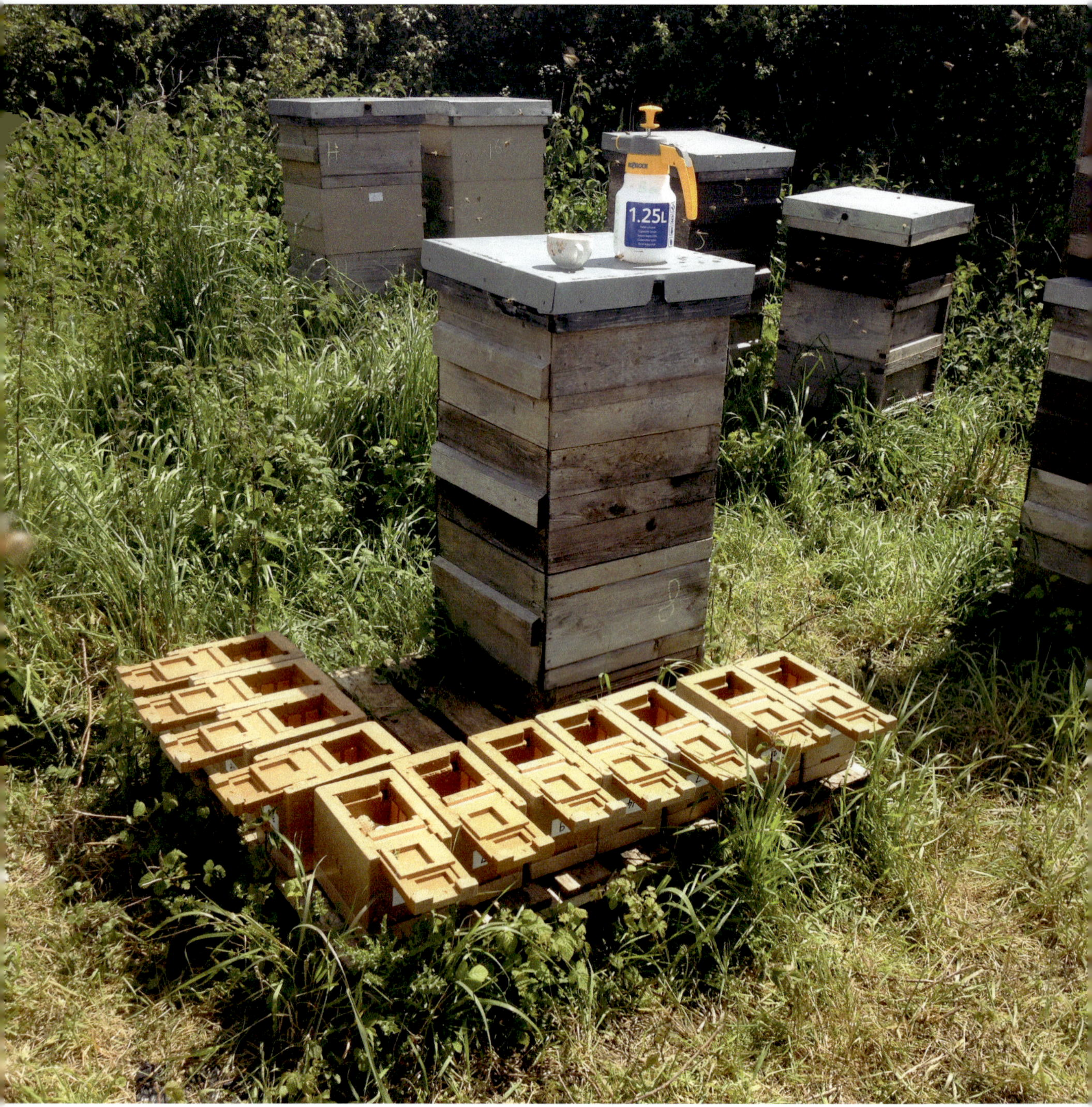
1.25L

3 Establishment

Once you have begun queen raising, it will soon be time to set up Apideas. Adding bees and a ripe queen cell to produce a cohesive little colony in a mini mating nuc is referred to as establishment, and is one of the much-anticipated milestones of each beekeeping season.

Establishment involves a number of activities which only need be performed when an empty mini-nuc is populated with bees. Once successfully established, you move into routine management of the mini-nuc, and then recycling after the first queen has been mated. When recycling an established mini-nuc (by removing a mated queen and introducing another ripe queen cell) the establishment tasks do not need to be performed again. Of course there are times when a mini-nuc has failed to establish successfully, or the population has dwindled to an unsustainable size due to repeated queen failure or loss, and it may be better to shake out the remaining bees and start again from scratch by re-establishing.

The principle underlining establishment could be described as using a shook swarm to make an artificial cast swarm. A number of worker bees are taken from their home colony, and placed together in a new hive with a ripe queen cell. They are disorientated by this process, and of course realise almost immediately that they have been separated from their familiar queen. By confining them for a few days whilst the ripe queen cell emerges and the young queen begins to mature, the workers adapt to the change in circumstances, adopting the young queen as their own and gaining cohesion as a colony, albeit a very small one.

The process of establishment can be summarised as follows: Apideas are assembled and laid out in an apiary with populous colonies. Workers are shaken from one colony into a collecting box, wetted with a fine water spray to prevent them from taking to the air, and then scooped into each of the waiting Apideas. A queen cell is added to each mini-nuc, and then the Apideas are stored in a cool dark

Using Apideas

place for three days before being released at dusk in the mating apiary. Once the bees have flown for a day and orientated to their new home and location, the Apideas can then be inspected and routine management begins.

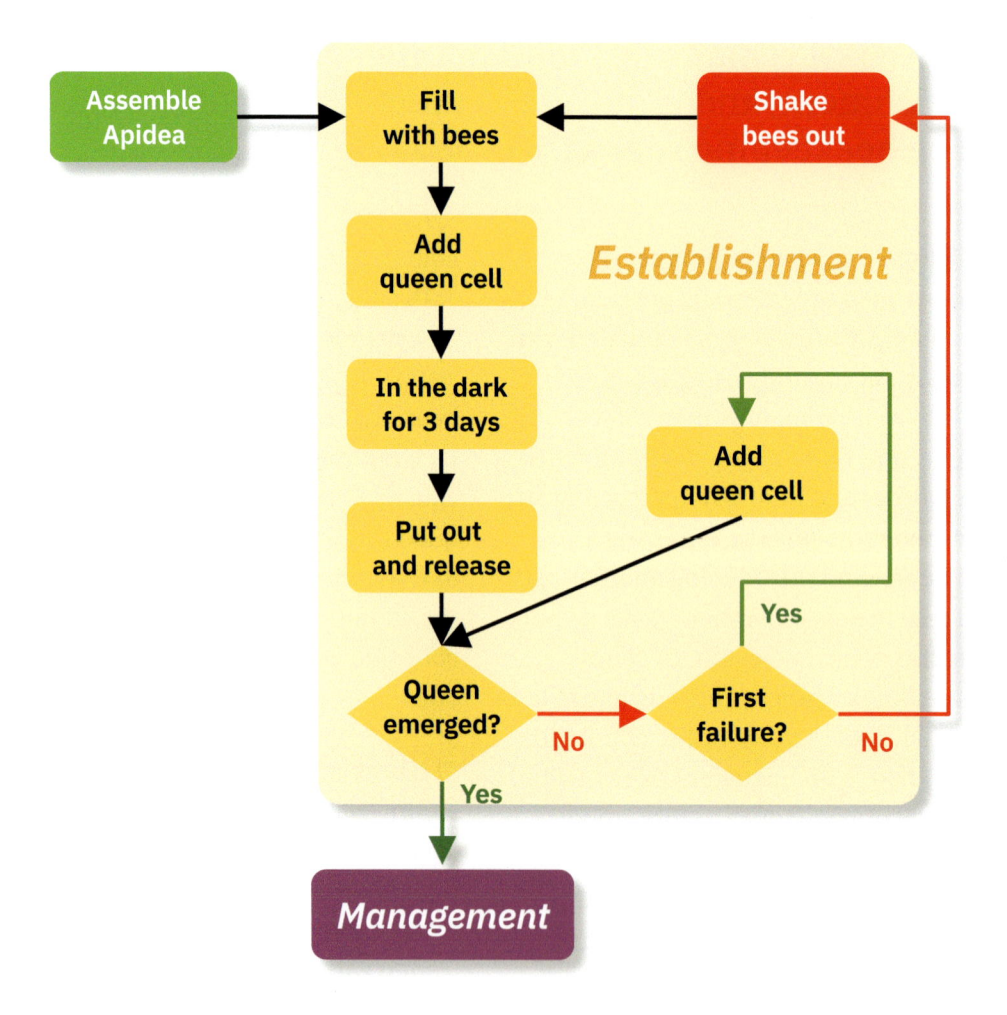

Establishment

Assemble Apidea → Fill with bees ← Shake bees out
Fill with bees → Add queen cell → In the dark for 3 days → Put out and release → Queen emerged?
Queen emerged? Yes → Management
Queen emerged? No → First failure?
First failure? Yes → Add queen cell → Fill with bees
First failure? No → Shake bees out

3.1 Pre-flight checks

Before setting out to establish Apideas, it's worth going through a quick mental checklist. This isn't just for the first time you ever use an Apidea – being a seasonal event, it's going to be at least eight months and possibly a year since you last did this, and details easily get forgotten in the intervening period.

If the bee shed, the colonies used to fill the Apideas with workers, and the queen raising colonies are all on one site, it's straightforward to nip off and get anything you've forgotten. Clearly it gets more complicated when your bee shed is not in the same apiary as the donor colonies and/or queen raising colonies, and you may be faced with the frustration of an additional round-trip in order to retrieve a crucial forgotten item.

Once in the apiary, it's important to have everything set up and ready to go before you start collecting workers. Collecting and filling needs to be fluid and seamless if you are to avoid losing the collected workers up into the air whilst you fiddle with forgotten entrance sliders or search for your filling cup.

If you are filling Apideas with workers in an apiary remote from your queen raisers, you'll fill a number of Apideas to accommodate the number of ripe queen cells noted in your queen raising records. When you arrive at the queen raising apiary, you might find that some of these filled Apideas are no longer needed. Those unwanted Apideas can simply be shaken out when back in the donor apiary, and their workers will return to their original colonies none the worse for wear.

Using Apideas

Establishment checks: shed

- ☐ Do you have enough Apideas to hand for the expected number of ripe queen cells?
- ☐ Are the Apideas completely assembled?
  - ☐ Are the red grille and feeder queen excluder in place?
  - ☐ Are the frames in and do they have starter strips in them?
  - ☐ Is there a new feed cartridge in the feeder, and does it have a cut lid?
  - ☐ Is the crownboard fitted with the flap/hole in the correct place?
  - ☐ Have you tested that your frames are correctly orientated to accommodate your queen cells?
  - ☐ Is there a pin in place to hold the entrance slider shut?
- ☐ Do you have the collecting box, cup, and water spray?
- ☐ Do you need to take a board or other flat surface to work on in the apiary?

Using Apideas, chapter 3: Establishment

Establishment checks: apiary

- [ ] Identify the donor colony (or colonies) you are taking workers from
- [ ] Double-check the number of ripe queen cells, i.e. the number of Apideas needed
- [ ] Are all entrance sliders pinned shut?
- [ ] Invert the Apideas on a flat surface, with their floors slid fully open
- [ ] Place the filling cup by the Apideas

Now begin collecting workers from donors...

3.2 Filling with bees

To stock mini-nucs with bees, there are two distinct processes, both of which are greatly facilitated by having two people working together. The first is the **collection** of workers from a donor colony, the second is the **distribution** of these workers into the waiting mini-nucs.

Both of these processes need a certain pace – not rushing clumsily, but working swiftly and smoothly – since they involve collecting, holding, and distributing worker bees who have an understandable desire to take flight. Once you have collected sufficient bees you will want to move quickly and seamlessly to distributing them into these waiting mini-nucs.

Before you begin collecting workers, ensure that your mini-nucs are laid out, upside down with entrances closed and floors slid wide open for filling with bees. Six Apideas can be safely arranged on a flat hive roof; for larger numbers we use a spare pallet on which to lay out two lines of inverted Apideas. In the absence of anything else, lay a spare crownboard on the ground to give a steady platform for six Apideas.

For the collecting box, we use a wooden nuc box with a permanently attached floor. This is robust enough to withstand the periodic knocking on the ground that is needed in order to contain and corral the bees within.

Usually both the collection and distribution of workers takes place in the same apiary. This may be your queen raising apiary, or you may have carefully transported ripe queen cells to a remote apiary where the mini-nucs are to be stocked.

3.2.1   Collecting workers

Identify a healthy donor colony, and work through the brood frames using minimal disturbance and smoke, looking for the queen. Cage her and place her safely on the top bars of the brood frames, or put her and the frame she is found on into a closed nuc box to hold her securely..

We use an ordinary hand-held pressurised garden sprayer, the sort that has a plunger on the top. We keep one marked up for use with the bees to ensure that it is never filled with anything other than clean water. Adjust the nozzle to give a fine mist spray.

Combs of bees can now be taken from a donor colony, lightly misted with cold water on both sides, and then the bees are shaken into the collecting box.

This collecting box can be periodically sprayed lightly with water to subdue the bees within and discourage them from taking flight. Do not soak the bees so that they are completely motionless, since this chills them unnecessarily. Knocking the box firmly against the ground will drop bees crawling up the walls back into the pool of bees at the bottom. Attempting to use a cover actually makes collection more clumsy and is more likely to result in crushing bees.

Most of the drones present will be gathered on the fringes of the brood nest - probably the outermost frames - and such frames can be skipped. Including the odd drone is not an issue unless you will be taking your mini-nucs to an isolated mating apiary.

This collection process will give you a pool of workers in the collecting box that are predominantly younger bees

Pressurised garden sprayer

We keep one of these marked up for beekeeping, only ever filled with clean water

Using Apideas

Collecting workers

The queen has been found and is in a cage, resting over the top bars of the donor colony.

Combs of bees are taken out, lightly sprayed with cold water on both sides ….

… and then the bees are shaken into a collecting box.

from the brood area. A strong colony will easily supply enough bees to stock a dozen Apideas without being heavily diminished; the bees taken represent around 4 days of peak brood laying / emergence. Do not collect from this colony again for a week, to allow its population time to recover.

If you are filling more than a dozen mini-nucs in one go, it's wise to have several donors earmarked so that you can take bees from each in turn. Amidst the confusion and disorientation of collection, wetted workers from different

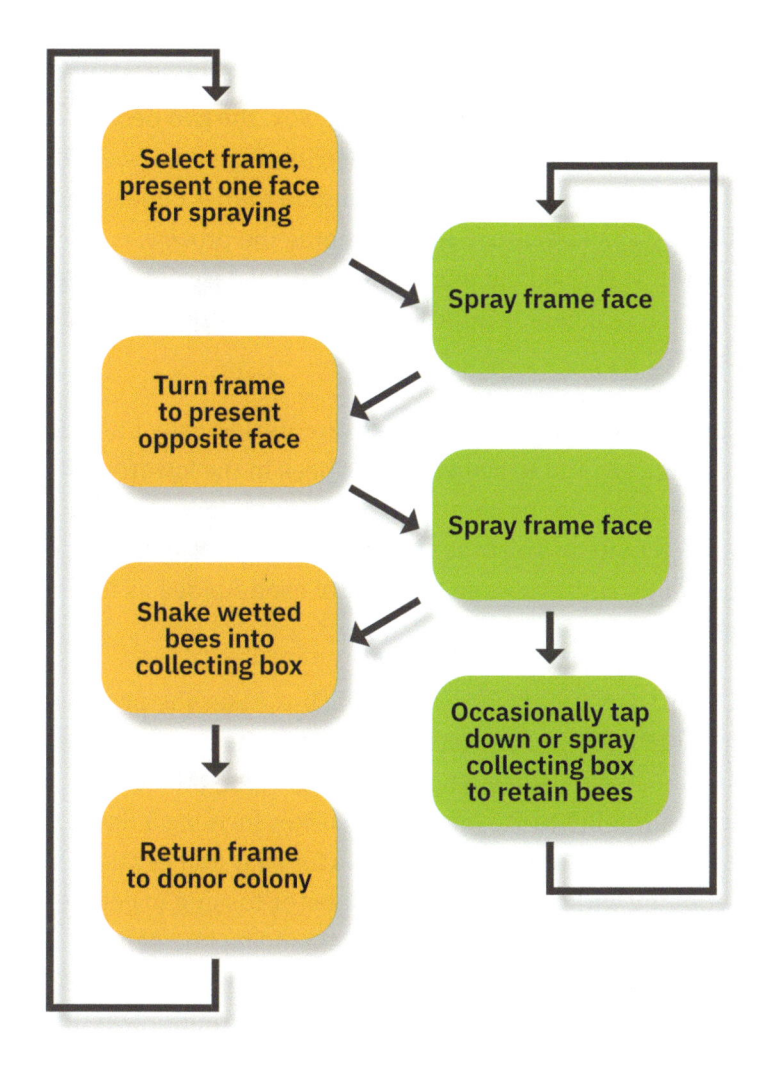

Collecting bees: the process with two people

The two columns indicate the overlapping actions of the two people. The orange column is for the person selecting and shaking frames, the green column for the person spraying with water and managing the collecting box.

Orange column (select and shake):
- Select frame, present one face for spraying
- Turn frame to present opposite face
- Shake wetted bees into collecting box
- Return frame to donor colony

Green column (spray and manage box):
- Spray frame face
- Spray frame face
- Occasionally tap down or spray collecting box to retain bees

colonies can be shaken together into the collecting box and will not fight.

This process really works better with two people working together: one to spray combs and manage the collecting box, the other to select brood combs, offer both sides for water spray, and then shake the bees into the collecting box.

Using Apideas

3.2.2 Distribution of workers into mini-nucs

With enough bees in the collecting box, the two people then switch to filling Apideas. Distribution of the bees is much more achievable single-handed than is collection, although as with much in beekeeping the process is slicker with a second person helping. I'll describe it here with the two person approach to clarify the sequence of tasks.

One person takes the collecting box, periodically knocking it on the ground to keep a pool of bees in the lowermost corner, and scoops bees from the box and into each Apidea in turn. The other person follows alongside, promptly sliding closed the floor of each Apidea as it is filled.

The management of the collecting box eases the process for both bees and beekeeper. The box is held at an angle such that, with a firm knock on the ground, the bees within will fall to the lowermost corner forming a deep but compact pool of bees. This allows for easy and gentle scooping without scraping the sides or fussing to get the last few bees into the cup. There should be no need for further water spray at this stage. The box is carried in this fashion in one hand along the line of mini-nucs, with the scoop held in the other hand.

As noted in Chapter 2 - *Getting Ready* - we use a simple thin-rimmed melamine camping cup of circa 250ml, or a cut-down one pint plastic milk bottle of the same volume, either of which contains just over 600 wetted live bees when filled level with the top. This is scooped through the pool of accumulated bees, and then a gentle side-to-side shake will remove any excess above the level of the rim.

Scooping from the pool of bees

By keeping a pool of wetted bees in the lowermost corner of the collecting box, we can easily scoop full cups of bees with minimal fuss.

Distributing workers

The scoop of bees has been shaken lightly from side-to-side over the collecting box to ensure it is filled level with bees ...

... the bees are then thrown smartly into a waiting Apidea, using a definite 'flick' which deposits them all in one go deep into the space.

Without pausing, the bees are then thrown into the next available open mini-nuc. This is not a pouring action, which has a tendency to end up with some bees in, some almost in, and some trying to get out. Rather, it is a definite flick of the scoop to ensure all the bees are thrown in at once onto the depths of the inverted mini-nuc.

The second person is on hand to close the floor of the just-filled mini-nuc as soon as the bees have been deposited. This again needs to be a swift, no-fiddling action, since bees may be crawling out within a second or two. Being

Distributing bees into mini-nucs

Again the two columns indicate the overlapping actions of two people, although this process is rather easier to complete single-handed. The orange column is for the person managing the collecting box and scooping bees, the green column for the person closing the mini-nuc floors.

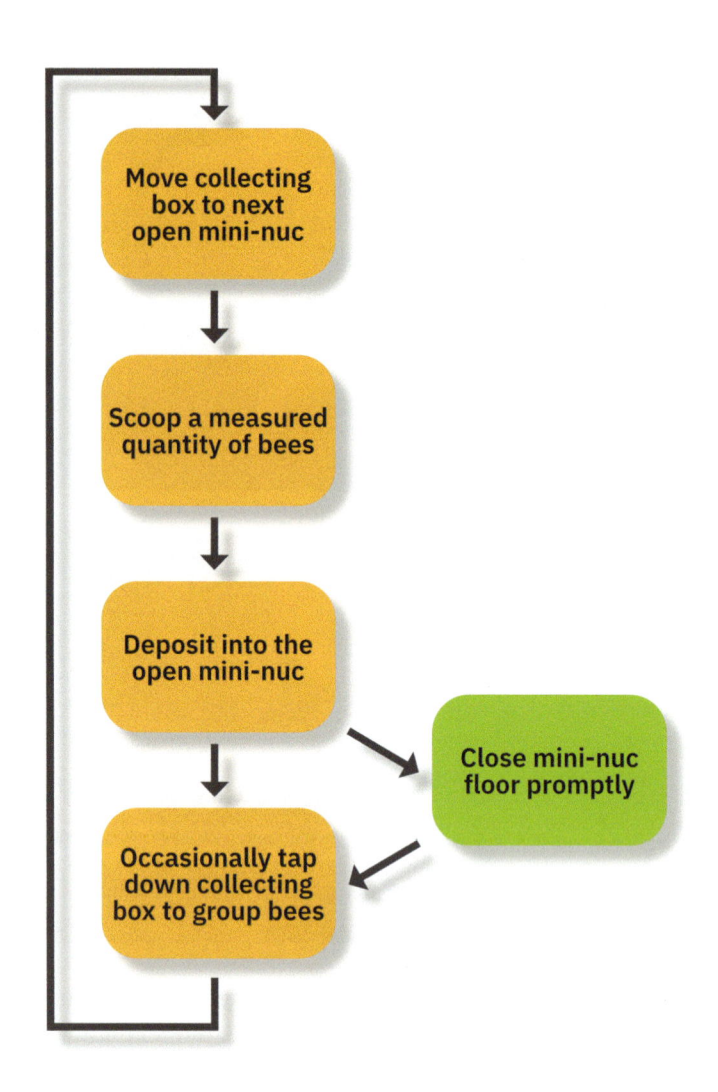

```
Move collecting box to next open mini-nuc
  ↓
Scoop a measured quantity of bees
  ↓
Deposit into the open mini-nuc
  ↓
Occasionally tap down collecting box to group bees  →  Close mini-nuc floor promptly
```

slow with the floor, then pausing to fluff a bee or two out of the way to avoid crushing, risks losing a flood of escaping bees. Provided the bees have been cleanly deposited by the first person, and the second person is quick with the floor, no bees should be crushed or lost.

It may seem as if this is a brutal operation: bees thrown into the bottom of the mini-nuc, and floors slamming shut on them. It is not; we are simply avoiding the disorientated bees' instinct to depart out to the light, by moving calmly but swiftly, because even a modest number of bees lost may have a significant impact on the viability of the mini-nuc population. The 'flick' action of depositing the bees out of the scoop need be no more abrupt than the 'stop' when shaking bees from a frame to inspect comb beneath them. Indeed the latter needs a more vigorous motion since the bees generally have a much better footing on comb than they do when scooped wetted into a smooth plastic cup.

If you have underestimated the number of bees that you need to fill the required number of mini-nucs, you will now need to go and collect more from another donor colony. Alternatively, if you have more wetted bees in the collecting box than were needed, it is best to return these to their original colony by shaking them back in under the crownboard. This is why it's preferable to collect from just one donor colony at a time, so there are no concerns over possibly returning foreign bees to a donor colony.

3.2.3 Turning mini-nucs the right way up

Having filled the mini-nucs with bees, now turn them back the right way up and ensure that entrance sliders remain closed. This then allows the roof to be lifted to insert a queen cell through the hole in the crownboard.

Be very careful when turning over filled mini-nucs. If you have larger hands, it may be possible to lift and turn over most Apidea-sized mini-nucs with just one hand. Unfortunately, the roof fits snugly right up to the point that it doesn't, tumbling frames, bees, bits of red plastic, and

Using Apideas

Turning Apideas over

Hold the Apidea securely with two hands (one under the floor and one over the roof) as you turn it right way up.

feeder and fondant onto the floor. You aren't going to scoop that lot back into the Apidea before half the bees have departed. Write it off. Shake out any remaining bees, assemble the Apidea once again, check the frame alignment, collect some more bees, and fill it again.

This is a particular problem with any used polystyrene mini-nucs - Apideas or clones - where the parts have loosened with age and wear. Swienty's Swi-Bine seems particularly prone to this in my experience. The safest way to turn over a mini-nuc is to hold it with two hands, one holding the roof and one holding the floor, then rotate the whole lot over, setting it down before letting go with either hand. Essentially you treat each mini-nuc as if it is going to tumble open if lifted with just one hand. It may sound a faff but it only adds a moment to the process; it's far quicker and much less effort than having to refill them!

Having got the mini-nucs the right way up, ensure that the entrance sliders are still firmly shut. If you are dealing with larger numbers of mini-nucs, ensure that they are grouped in such a way that the entrance grilles, although exposed, are not pressed up to an adjacent mini-nuc in any way that would prevent adequate ventilation. Best to arrange them in separate lines.

3.2.4 More selective collection of workers

If you are particularly concerned about the ages of workers taken, or by the inclusion of drones, then you need to take additional preparatory steps at least a couple of hours before you plan to collect bees from a colony. The aim is to take a strong colony and arrange an upper brood box of predominantly open brood, with all bees shaken off those frames, and sandwich this between queen excluders. Young workers will be drawn into this space and can then be collected.

Arrange a second brood box and a pair of queen excluders. Find the queen and put her aside, then shake all the bees off each comb of open brood found in the bottom brood box, transferring the bee-less combs into the second brood box. Cover this second box as you work to shade the combs and so that bees do not alight on them. You will progressively fill this second box with open brood frames cleared of bees.

In the lower brood box, group and centralise the remaining sealed brood frames and surround with additional frames, ideally with some empty drawn comb for immediate laying space. Release the queen into the lower brood box, then place a queen excluder over the top. Put your bee-free second box of open brood on top of the queen excluder, the second queen excluder over this box, and replace the supers above.

As the colony normalises in the hours after the manipulation, young workers are drawn to the brood frames in order to attend to the brood; the queen and any drones will be excluded. You now have a donor colony where the upper brood box contains young workers, few or no foragers, and no drones. Knowing that the queen is in the lower brood box means that you can begin shaking workers into your collecting box without the disruption of first working through to find her.

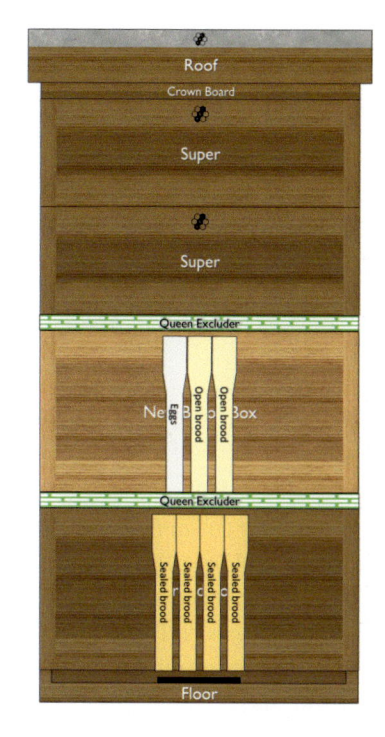

Selective collection of workers

Open brood is sandwiched between queen excluders in the new brood box. This upper brood box soon contains young workers, no foragers, and no queen or drones, providing an ideal source of young workers for stocking mini-nucs.

Using Apideas

3.3 Queen cell introduction

Retrieve your ripe queen cells, separating each one in turn from its comb, cell bar, or whatever. Lift off an Apidea roof, open the flap, and promptly offer the queen cell down into the gap between the frames before bees emerge. Ensure the queen cell is securely suspended, and that the plastic flap does not flip back over it as the roof is replaced, otherwise the queen cell may be pushed down and drop to the floor, failing to emerge. This can be a problem when Apideas are new, as the sticker 'hinge' on the flap is particularly springy and readily jumps back into the 'closed' position unless positive pressure is maintained on it.

To achieve this, I work from the front of the Apidea, holding the roof with one hand such that I can read the APIDEA script on top and the roof is about an inch forward of the hive body. This ensures that one of the large round cut-outs in the underside of the roof will be aligned over the queen cell, preventing the roof from contacting the

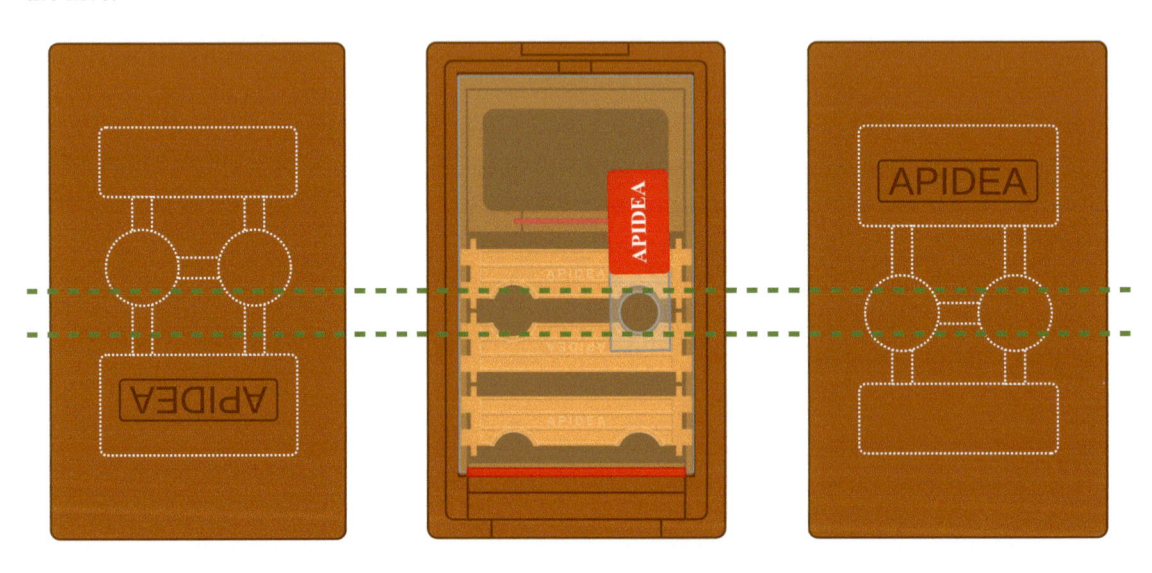

Aligning the roof

The circular cut-outs in the underside of the roof (shown as dotted white lines) only fit correctly one way. To ensure clearance for the queen cell, the roof should always be placed so that the moulded APIDEA script is the right way up when looking at the front of the hive.

3 Establishment

Safe return of roof over queen cell

Bring the roof down until it contacts the opened flap, then sweep the roof back and down until it is snugly in place. This pushes the flap backwards and prevents it from springing back over the queen cell.

queen cell and possibly pushing it downwards. The other hand is holding the flap away from the queen cell carrier. Bring the roof down until it contacts the flap, and so prevents it from springing back over the cell carrier. Now sweep the roof back and down in a smooth movement until it is snugly in place, so that the flap is naturally pressed safely away from that queen cell carrier.

3.3.1 Candling queen cells

Most of the queen raising texts talk of 'candling' ripe queen cells, by holding them up against a bright light source (such as the sun) and looking for movement within. Because I generally move queen cells on at day 14, my experience is that, whilst it is easy to differentiate between filled and empty queen cells, it is rare to detect any obvious movement on this day, even in perfectly viable queen cells. Check a day later and the moving queen is more readily apparent, but you're not leaving much in the way of a contingency as regards emergence timings. Remember the variability of larval age at selection and

Using Apideas

Candling queen cells

Both the Jenter/Cupkit and JZBZ cell carriers are transparent enough for 'candling' of queen cells. A dark body is apparent in filled, ripe cells, and it is obvious that the centre cell is failed or empty.

variability of development timings due to environmental factors, both of which will have a bearing on the precise hour of that emergence "during day 15".

Instead, I check ripe queen cells by holding them inverted (tip upwards) between thumb and second finger, and very delicately shaking them side-to-side to feel for the queen moving to and fro within. Any cell with no apparent movement is discarded – opening it generally reveals an empty cell, a decaying larva/pupa, or a mix-up that has resulted in much younger unripe cells being selected by mistake!

Gently shaking to check queen cell contents

A very gentle side-to-side shake of a queen cell held between thumb and second finger. If there is a pupa within, you will feel her move from side to side. If the cell is empty, no movement will be felt. I find this is more useful that the traditional candling.

3.4 Storing in the dark

Newly established mini-nucs should be stored, entrances closed, in a cool dark place for three days to allow the bees within to achieve cohesion as a colony. As discussed in section 2.1.3, *When to add queen cells*, my preference is to include the queen cell during this confinement, to increase the chances of cohesion. This confinement is only required at set-up of the mini-nuc, and is not necessary if the mini-nuc has been established and free-flying for some time, e.g. when adding a new queen cell after having removed a previously mated queen from that same mini-nuc.

It is important during this confinement period that the mini-nuc does not overheat, that sufficient ventilation is available to the bees, and that food and water are available. Ideally exposure to light should be kept to a minimum, since this audibly excites (and likely frustrates) the bees within.

Avoid the temptation to put the mini-nuc somewhere obviously warm, like an airing cupboard or an under-stairs cupboard, particularly if there is a number of mini-nucs to be confined at the same time. The insulating properties of the polystyrene, combined with the higher ambient temperature and likely poor ventilation of the cupboard will do more harm than good. The back of a domestic garage, facing towards the wall, would generally be an ideal store – a steady cool temperature, and mostly dark.

Keep a small spray bottle of tap water with the confined mini-nucs, and use this to give 2-3 good squirts of water across the large red ventilation grille morning and

Twenty four Apideas stored in the dark

Keeping the closed Apideas in a dark space reduces the apparent stress on the bees, who will roar and mass at the grilles when a light is turned on, then subdue shortly after the light is turned out.

Grilles accessible and clean water spray kept nearby

Turn the Apideas so that it is easy to spray water across the grilles. Here they are stored in a shower room that is dark as soon as the door is closed, but well ventilated.

evening. Adjust the nozzle to give a fine spray – the objective is not to hose the inhabitants, but to deposit small water droplets across the grille. Label this spray as "Bees Only" or similar, and ensure it only ever has clean water in it – even mildly soapy water will be fatal.

If tempted to re-use an old spray cleaner bottle or similar, rinse it thoroughly (including pumping much water through the spray mechanism) until it is clear of any detergent residue. Tasting a small amount of the water it dispenses gives a much more sensitive measure than trying to ascertain remaining 'soapiness' by touch or smell.

In/out cards

Taking Apideas out after three days in the dark sounds straightforward until you forget when you put them in the dark! The in/out cards aim to make this foolproof - by having the corresponding 'in' and 'out' days printed on each side.

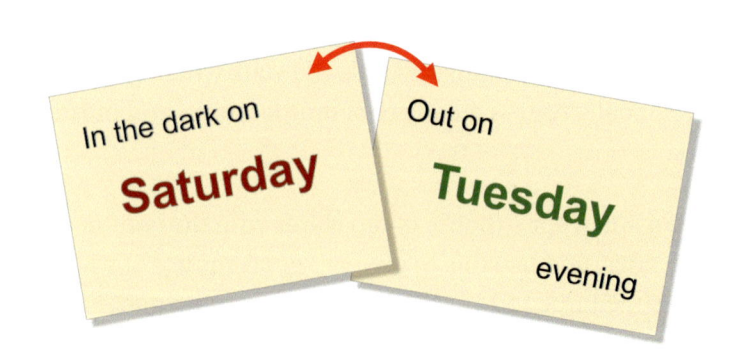

To help ensure that the stored Apideas are indeed put out after three days in the dark, I have made up some simple 'in/out cards'. These are printed on two sides, one side showing the day going into storage, the other side showing the corresponding day to come out. I simply select today's day on the 'in' side, flip the card over and place on top of the stack of Apideas so that the correct 'out' day is shown.

It may sound like overkill, but it brings the reassurance of a positive marking, and is particularly useful during peak beekeeping in May when the days tend to blur together, or when you have two overlapping batches of Apideas going into and out of storage on different days.

Details of how to download and print the in/out cards are given in Chapter 12, *Resources*.

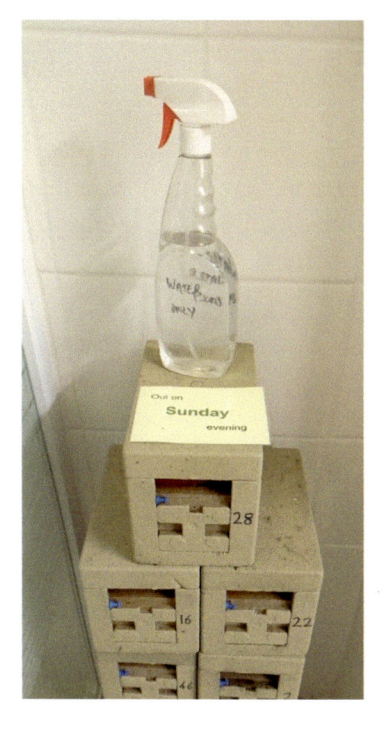

Water spray and in/out cards

We store small numbers of Apideas in the shower room in the honey house - it is rarely used, well ventilated, and dark. A water spray is kept in this room solely for watering the Apideas, marked 'water only'. Also shown is the in/out card usage - these Apideas were put in the dark on Thursday, so the 'in on Thursday' card was chosen and flipped over to show the correct 'out' day.

Using Apideas

3.5 Putting Apideas out at dusk

After three days of confinement, newly established mini-nucs should be put out at dusk. This timing allows for a gentle emergence and orientation for the occupants at the following dawn, as per any hive moved to a new location. Prepare your stands during the daytime, though, and assemble sufficient roof weights conveniently, rather than fumbling in the dark.

If the queen has emerged successfully, a confined mini-nuc will usually have achieved such cohesion that it can be put out in the same apiary from which its constituent workers were taken. This is quite remarkable, and clearly breaks the "three feet or three miles" rule of thumb. I liken the process of mini-nuc stocking and confinement to that of swarming in this respect: the act (or belief) of colony division appears to provide a powerful reset for the homing instinct of honey bees.

Putting Apideas out at dusk

A wildlife camera records Apideas being put out in the mating apiary at dusk. The bees will be drawn out gradually by the dawn light, and will orientate successfully. Much better than having them tumbling out chaotically if opened in the daytime.

If, however, the queen cell has failed to emerge, the workers lack that cohesive sense of a colony, and will quickly disperse or abscond once released. This is particularly the case if the mini-nuc is put out in the apiary from which it was stocked.

When positioning the mini-nucs, remember the usual practices about trying to vary the pattern and orientation of mini-nucs. Whilst it is tempting to squeeze in as many as you can, having entrances too close, or indeed facing each other, can bring about special problems of queen disorientation during mating flights. Queenless colonies will sense the mating flight activity of nearby colonies, and opportunist workers may fan to attract another colony's returning queen to resolve their queenlessness.

Arranging mini-nucs

This table has been improvised from a full sheet of plywood supported by spare brood boxes. It gives ample space for arranging twenty Apideas alongside each other, whilst providing good working spaces and minimising adjacent or facing entrances.

3.6 Checking for queen emergence

Once a newly-established mini-nuc has had a day of flying after having been put out in the apiary, you can safely inspect. Initially, a quick peep under the roof should show whether all is good, and allow you to withdraw the queen cell to check for emergence.

If the queen has indeed emerged and all appears fine then we move into the routine **management** phase as described in the next chapter.

If, however, the queen cell has not emerged, then we must assess the state of the mini-nuc to decide what to do with it next. The key question is whether sufficient workers remain in order to host another ripe queen cell. Many workers may be gathered in the feeder compartment - a classic indicator of failure to emerge - but some may have drifted away to adjacent queenright mini-nucs or colonies. By lifting the crownboard and checking both the frames and the feed compartment, you will learn to judge whether sufficient workers remain. It is useful to compare populations in failed and successful mini-nucs.

If the population is sufficient, another ripe queen cell should be given to this mini-nuc as soon as possible. Day by day the population will dwindle if no queen or queen cell is present. Workers steadily disperse to the more appealing queenright mini-nucs nearby. I work on the basis that an Apidea gets two chances. If the second queen cell given does not emerge, that Apidea is shaken out and re-stocked from scratch - a third attempt is almost certain to waste a good ripe queen cell.

Failed, but try again

Finding the bees camped in the feeder is a sure sign that the queen failed to emerge. Here both the feed compartment and area between it and frame 3 appear to be well filled with workers so I would confidently add another ripe queen cell in here today or tomorrow.

Regardless of the success or failure of emergence, pull the queen cell out promptly. If it is left in place for any longer than necessary, the queen cell will become braced and incorporated into the newly-drawn combs, regardless of outcome. This makes queen cell removal difficult and can result in warped or damaged combs on both frames 2 and 3.

Queen cell left in too long

When a queen cell is left in too long, not only can it be heavily braced to the fragile comb, but it can distort comb drawing on frames 2 & 3. Better to remove queen cells promptly after anticipated emergence, with an early check of success or failure.

91

4 Management

Once an Apidea has been successfully established, it needs ongoing management as a small queen mating colony that may not be sustainable without intervention. This is a subset of normal colony management, tailored to the specific purpose and vulnerabilities of a recently established mini mating nuc.

4.1 Timing of inspections

Queens take mating flights during the warmest part of the day, usually mid-afternoon. It is unwise to inspect mating hives of any sort whilst queens are taking mating flights, as the disruption and disorientation caused may result in a queen returning to the wrong colony.

I have made this mistake and witnessed a mating queen return to the wrong, open, and very much queenright Apidea, whereupon she was immediately and fatally balled by hostile workers. If you can, intercept the balled queen quickly, free her from the ball of workers with smoke or water and throw her high up into the air, then quickly close the open mating hive and walk away. That at least gives her the chance to re-orientate on her own hive, and is a more elegant solution than trying to hold her whilst you guess which mating hive she came from. Even worse would be to open other mating hives to check for an absent queen, since that would exacerbate the 'mating hives open whilst queens are returning' problem.

Observation has shown midday to 4pm to be the active mating window for my climate. Thus I impose a curfew on mini-nuc inspections: they must be completed before midday, or started after 4pm. My preference is to inspect from 9am until midday, since as with any other colony the absence of a foraging workforce allows one to work more quickly and find the queen more readily. You will be surprised (and embarrassed!) at how difficult it can be sometimes to spot a queen in a busy Apidea.

Using Apideas

Due to the developmental timetable of queen raising, some manipulations of the Apideas may need to take place in wet weather. If this is the case, it is of great benefit to have an assistant who can hold an umbrella over the open colony; remember that the beekeeper's comfort should always be secondary to that of the bees!

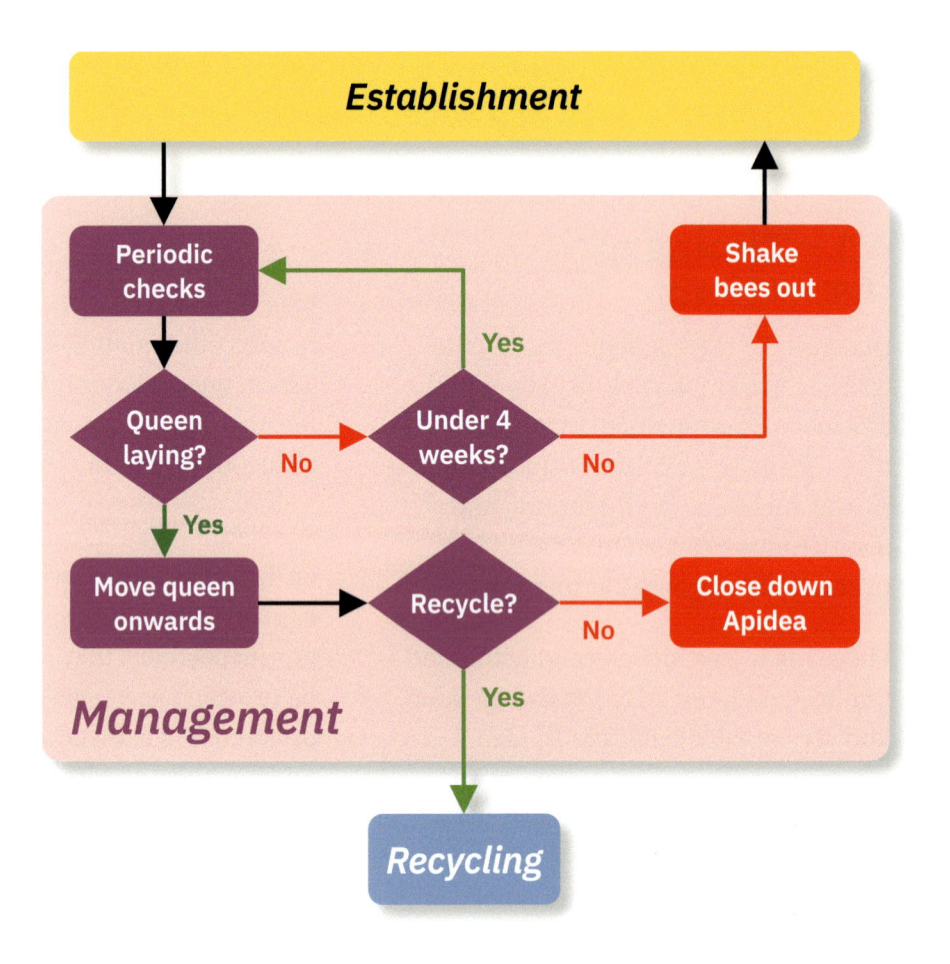

Establishment

Management

- Periodic checks
- Queen laying?
  - No → Under 4 weeks?
    - Yes → Periodic checks
    - No → Shake bees out
  - Yes → Move queen onwards → Recycle?
    - No → Close down Apidea
    - Yes → *Recycling*

4.2   Inspecting Apideas

In our production hives, we run populous colonies over multiple single-depth boxes. Most colonies run double brood, some triple brood, plus deep supers. We have adopted an approach to disassembling a hive for inspection that both allows us access to the various boxes - because we may wish to exchange frames between any two boxes - and to reassemble the hive in the correct order by default. Upturned roofs are used to support removed boxes, and boxes are placed in order leading towards the hive stand so that the supers are furthest away, second brood box nearest. This way, the original box order is always apparent. Importantly, the approach is so well practised that it is instinctive, and therefore one less distraction from the pleasures of beekeeping.

The same approach helps with Apideas; both in the use of upturned roofs and in working methodically in the often confined space of the mating apiary tables. The key, I believe, is to unpack an Apidea into its own upturned roof. This provides a compact and stable platform for the removed frames, and despite having a minimal edge boundary is surprisingly effective at retaining an overlooked queen, who much prefers the shade between frames anyway.

The inverted Apidea frames stand quite stable except on the windiest of days. Their design usefully incorporates a beespace in the side bar / top bar joint, so no need to worry about squashing any bees. With such small colonies, brood can easily become isolated if frames are mixed up during inspection. By always arranging the removed frames in the same order, you can see at a glance which frame was where, and re-pack in the same order if

Using Apideas

no further management is required.

Colonies love the warmth of the frame closest to the feeder, and this is where comb drawing and brood raising begins - and where a probably-still-flighty young queen is likely to be found. The frame closest to the entrance is generally a stores frame and thus a very good candidate for a safe first frame out, allowing for a gentle approach to the remaining frames.

The procedure is as follows:

1. Take off the roof and turn upside down, placing next to or behind the Apidea in question (but not in the direct flight line of another);

2. Take off the crown board, turn upside down, and place within the roof;

3. Lift out the frame closest to the entrance, check carefully for the queen and then for any eggs, and place it upside down (resting on its top bar) on the crown board;

4. Repeat for each of the remaining frames;

It is most likely that the first egg laying will take place on the frame furthest from the entrance - the frame adjacent to the feeder compartment in the standard 3-frame layout.

Note that each frame should be checked first for the queen, then for eggs. This will run against your instinct, which naturally has you wanting to peer into each comb as soon as it is withdrawn in order to spot those precious eggs - indicators of another success. By doing so, you may overlook a small, flighty queen who is not yet quite ready

Removing frames

The upturned roof makes a stable platform for standing removed frames inverted. Start nearest to the entrance, and arrange frames so that their original position is clear.

95

to lay, and she may well take to the air. Instead, check each frame first for the queen, and only switch to looking for eggs when you have satisfied yourself that she is not on this frame. Queens move around, brood stays put.

If at any point a young queen is spotted I halt the inspection and immediately re-assemble the Apidea. It may be apparent from her movement that she is young and flighty, or from the record sheets that it is too soon for her to have been mated. The record sheet is marked as 'VQS', standing for 'virgin queen seen', so that I know she was still present. Queens do get lost on mating flights, probably either to disorientation or to the birds.

If you are searching in vain for a laying queen, it can be very useful to pick up the open Apidea whilst all frames are out and tilt it so that sunlight shines on the floor, the corners, and all inner walls in turn. This can help greatly in finding that shy queen. However, queens love to hide in the entrance niche, often running between the inner and outer reaches of the entrance to avoid the light. Gently slide a little finger into this entrance hole from the outside – unless you have impolite bees they will simply move aside – and you will remove the opportunity for a queen to hide here or, far worse, to fall out.

The removal of the feeder compartment should be avoided at all times. Even the slimmest beespace created by accidental lifting of the feeder will be of great interest to the bees, who will rush in to explore, and you can't be certain that the queen didn't slip in with them. It is then necessary to remove the feeder and the floor slide almost completely in order to brush the bees back out of harm's way, an activity that has all the hallmarks of herding cats.

Using Apideas

4.2.1 Lifting propolised frames

Where Apideas are regularly inspected, the frames can usually be withdrawn without resorting to a hive tool. However you will occasionally come across a particularly 'sticky' Apidea, prone to propolising, or perhaps one that hasn't been disturbed for longer than normal. In both cases, a hive tool is needed to separate and lift out the frames. With a simple methodical approach this can be done quickly, easily, and without damage to the polystyrene.

Look closely at the moulded polystyrene frame supports within the hive body and it is clear that they are a form of castellated runners, in addition to the frames themselves having Hoffman-style self-spacing side bars. When frames get stuck down, those moulded polystyrene castellations prevent them being eased sideways to loosen them.

J-tool partially inserted

It is not necessary to insert the J end of the tool all the way in between frames; this could damage combs. Resting the curve on top of the adjacent frame gives sufficient purchase to gently lever one frame against another.

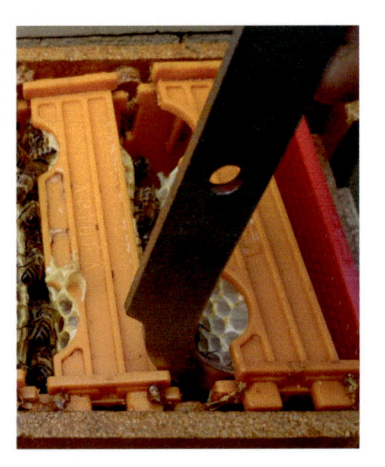

This belt-and-braces approach to frame spacing was probably chosen because it holds frames very securely during transport, which is likely to occur more frequently given the usage of mating nucs. Indeed in some European countries it is common for mini-nucs to be transported to remote or isolated mating apiaries in order to achieve a desirable mating outcome.

The polystyrene of the hive body is easily damaged by levering against it with a metal hive tool. Instead, use the J-end of a slender J-tool partially slipped between the frames, just inboard of the side bars. Do not slip the J-end all the way in - it's not necessary to rest the notch of the tool on the adjacent frame, and doing so might force the end of the J-tool through the comb on the frame you are trying to lift.

4 Management

Lifting propolised frames

Lift frame 1 by resting the curve of the J-tool on top of frame 2.

Lift frame 2 by resting on top of frame 3.

Turn the tool around, then **lift frame 3** by resting on top of frame 2.

All frames are thus freed without levering against the softer hive body with the J-tool, and should be easy to lift now by fingertips alone.

98

Gently lever one frame up against another frame, as shown. It is only necessary to lift the frames 5mm or so with the tool in order to break the propolis glue; they can subsequently be lifted manually.

All frames are thus quickly released without any levering against the polystyrene parts. With practice the movement becomes instinctive.

4.3 Feeding

Even strong Apidea populations are so small that their survival can be precarious in the British climate. Feeders should be kept stocked with fondant at all times, and checked on a weekly basis.

Using the fondant cartridge approach to feeding as described earlier, the fondant may last for around three weeks of poor spring or summer weather, when it is essential to the colony's survival. It is not wise to wait for a cartridge to be completely emptied before replacing it with a full one – the reserves present in an Apidea during poor weather can be awfully meagre compared to the needs of the colony. Instead swap out feed cartridges as soon as they are less than a third full. Unconsumed fondant is usually still pliable at this stage and can be recycled out of several cartridges to make one full one, assuming that your Apideas are equally healthy.

Using the notch at the rear of the Apidea hive body, flex the rear of the crownboard upwards and apply a little puff

Replace these feeders now!

Swap out old feeders when they are less than a third full. These shown should not be relied upon for more than a day or two. The fondant remnants can be collected together into one feeder to prevent wastage.

Using Apideas

Lift up the crownboard to access the feeder

Apply a puff of smoke as you lift the crownboard. You may choose to flex it upwards as shown, or remove it altogether.

of smoke. If the colony is established, the crownboard may be propolised to the frame tops but it will flex upwards in situ allowing you to access the feeder even if you do not wish to remove the crownboard completely.

When swapping feed cartridges, they are often stuck down by wax or propolis within the polystyrene feeder's aperture. Ensure that the removable feeder does not lift (and risk crushing bees beneath) by holding the feeder in

Hold down the feeder whilst changing feed cartridges

Often the feed cartridge is propolised into place, and will lift the feeder compartment unless this is held down.

Feed check on a rainy day

During wet weather, ensure all mini-nucs are checked and fed regularly. Here full feed cartridges are placed on each Apidea before a feed check. This helps speeds up checking and replacement on a rainy day, and ensures that none are missed.

place with one hand whilst lifting the cartridge with the other hand.

I greatly prefer to prepare my cartridges of feed indoors, at a table, with water to wash hands and tools, than to end up in a mess in the apiary. Having travelled with 12.5Kg fondant boxes, a large kitchen knife, and a rinsing bucket of clean water for the inevitable stickiness, it is so much more convenient instead just to carry pre-packaged feed!

During periods of poor weather when the mini-nucs are active, ensure that at the very minimum you do a weekly feed check. This may mean that you need to briefly open the mini-nucs on cold or rainy day - better that than risk starving. If you lift each mini-nuc before opening it, it becomes rapidly apparent which are light and in need of feed and which have good food reserves.

4.4 Handling queens

Until egg laying has started in an Apidea, a young queen will be particularly flighty, and there is nothing to be gained from trying to pick her up. Once egg laying has begun, the queen will be more docile and should be located and clipped and marked ready for moving onwards.

I prefer the approach to picking which is to immobilise the bee by light pressure of thumb and forefinger on the thorax, then pinch the fingertips together to pick up one or more wings as secure handles. Practice with drones until proficient!

The process is as follows, assuming that you are right-handed:

> **Hold the frame** in your left hand
>
> **Steer the queen** (or rotate the frame) so that ideally she is heading slowly from right to left across the comb.
>
> With light pressure from the thumb and forefinger, press down on the queen's thorax to **immobilise her** against the comb. Do not apply pressure to the abdomen.
>
> **Pinch your thumb and forefinger** together across the top of the queen's thorax, and you should be firmly holding her by one or both pairs of wings.
>
> You can **lift the queen** safely away from the comb.

4 Management

Picking up a queen by her wings

With **light pressure** from the thumb and forefinger, press down on the queen's thorax to **immobilise her** against the comb. Do not apply pressure to the abdomen.

Pinch your thumb and forefinger together across the top of the queen's thorax, and you should now be firmly holding her by one or both pairs of wings. You can lift her safely away from the comb

As you **lift the queen**, she will flail her legs as if looking for something to hold.

Using Apideas

Transferring to a leg hold

Offer up the forefinger of your left hand under her legs, and she will quickly grip your finger with them

Close the thumb of your left hand across the forefinger gripped by those legs, and ensure that you are holding at least two legs

Release the wings - you are now holding the queen by her legs with the thumb and forefinger of your left hand, leaving your right hand free for delicate clipping and marking.

If you wish to continue to clip and mark the queen, you need to transfer her to the other hand an in so doing expose her wings and the top of her thorax. Continue as follows:

> Lift the queen and she will flail her legs; put down the frame and **offer up the forefinger** of your left hand under her legs, and she will grip your finger

> **Close the thumb** of your left hand across the forefinger gripped by those legs, and ensure that you are holding at least two legs.

> **Release the wings** - you are now holding the queen by her legs with the thumb and forefinger of your left hand, leaving your right hand free for delicate clipping and marking.

It is important that you hold the queen by at least two legs, so that she cannot twist, which may result in leg damage. Do not grip so hard as to crush her legs, as these can be dislocated at the joints through excess pressure.

Pick and hold queens without wearing gloves and you will feel when adequate pressure is applied, both to immobilise against the comb and then to hold by the legs. Unless you have previously been dabbling bare-handed in diesel or some similarly pungent oil, do not worry about the effect of skin oils on the subsequent acceptance or rejection of the queen when she is returned to the colony - another of those beekeeping myths!

4.4.1 Picking a queen out of an Apidea

If the queen is found on a frame, she is easy to pick up. If, however, she is intent on running around on the Apidea floor or walls and you have even moderate sized hands, you will find it difficult to pick her up.

Just at the point that your fingertips close in on her, your hand obscures your view and so she is often missed. With practice it is possible to pick queens 'blind' despite this, especially without gloves, but getting sufficient practice to pick an obscured queen can be painful and frustrating for the beekeeper, and crushing for the bees. I can't think of any of the 'queen grabbers' sold by the equipment suppliers that would help in this circumstance.

As long as you are pursuing a mated, laying queen the solution is simple, if a little radical: knock the whole Apidea population out into an upturned hive roof and pick up the queen whilst the bees are sorting themselves out on the flat surface.

Don't try this with a flighty unmated queen since she will likely take to the air before you can catch her!

Be calm and confident with your queen picking, since even a mated queen will run faster with each failed attempt and may well take to the wing after three or four botched attempts.

Once you have picked and dealt with the queen, return the Apidea body to its familiar position and re-stock with frames. Knock any bees remaining in the roof into its corner, then tap them out in front of their Apidea.

This sounds particularly disruptive but the bees will

4 Management

Knocking out an Apidea to pick up a queen

Take a standard hive roof and place it nearby, upside down to act as a shallow container.

Remove all the frames from the Apidea if you have not already done so.

Holding the Apidea body at the feeder end, invert it over the upturned roof and tap the upper rim of the entrance end sharply down **once only**.

Examine the bees in the upturned roof and pick up the queen quickly but calmly.

108

Using Apideas

quickly right themselves afterwards. It removes a great deal of faff and fiddling in trying to extricate a shy queen from the innards of a small polystyrene box. By doing so, it greatly reduces the risk of injury to the queen... as long as you only tap the Apidea down once to spill the bees into the upturned hive roof. Tap it several times and you will be crushing bees.

4.4.2 Queen introduction cages

I find Swienty's 'puzzle' style of plastic queen cage (rectangular, interlocking) to be very convenient and well-designed as a queen introduction cage. Various similar patterns are available, with minor detail differences. Importantly for me, the Swienty cage has a hinged release flap so can be re-used (or indeed used as a holding cage during general inspections) and survives repeated washing in washing soda (see Chapter 10, *Maintenance*).

Introduction cages need to be prepared with a fondant plug at the appropriate end (to delay release) before the queen is added. You should also include 4-6 of the queen's workers to attend to her. I pick workers who are stationary or head-down in cells in the brood areas on the Apidea frames, avoiding fluffy youngsters and drones, neither of which is particularly suited to attending to the queen.

If there is any uncertainty about the destination of the queen, write the mini-nuc number on the cage with a 2B or chinagraph pencil. This will allow for the queen to be returned to her original mini-nuc should something not go to plan. This is discussed below in section 4.4.5, *Queen re-introduction*.

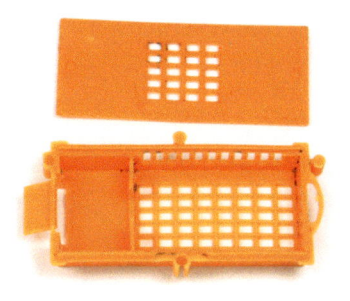

Swienty 'puzzle' cage

A classic amongst the various plastic queen introduction cages. No frills, good hanging loop, easy-to-slide cover, and the flap stays attached so that the cage can be re-closed and re-used many times.

4.4.3 Caging queens with workers

The process for caging is very straightforward, but requires some dexterity. Slide the cover of the introduction cage open by a generous beespace, and practice covering and uncovering the slot by rolling a thumb across it. You will use this motion to calmly contain each bee as she is introduced, and it is important that you neither squash the bees nor lose them back out of the cage. I am right-handed, so I hold the cage in my left hand and use my left thumb for covering the slot.

First cage the queen. Pick her by a wing (as described earlier) and rotate her into the slot of the cage, abdomen first until she is face-down. Roll your thumb over her to gently encourage her down into the cage.

Once she is safely in, turn your attention to the workers. Lay a populous brood comb horizontally, and pick the workers as you would a queen - light pressure on the thorax with thumb and forefinger to immobilise, then a pinching action of the fingertips to pick up by a wing. If you are right handed, selecting workers that are traversing from right to left on the comb helps with picking them up, *vice versa* for left handed beekeepers. Be swift and decisive, but not brutal. As long as you grip a worker's wing close to the root, she cannot twist to sting you. Just as for the queen, roll your thumb back from the slot and feed the worker in, abdomen first, rolling your thumb back into place to cover the opening.

When all the required bees are in the cage, slide the cover closed. Do this in two stages - closed to just a millimetre gap, check carefully that no legs, antennae, or wings are protruding, then fully close the cover. If necessary, cover

Caging queen and workers

Slide the lid of the introduction cage open by a generous beespace, and cover with your other thumb.

Holding the queen by her wings, rotate her sting-first into the cage whilst rolling back your thumb to uncover the gap …

… position the queen so that she is face down and fully in the cage before releasing your grip of her wings …

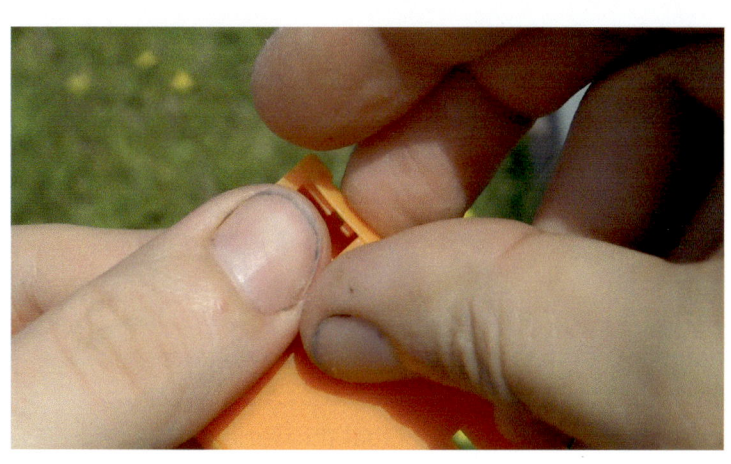

… as you release the queen's wings, roll your other thumb gently but promptly over the gap to contain her and encourage her to walk down in to the cage.

The same process is now repeated to add 5 or 6 workers into the cage. Add them sting-first, and it will be rare that your thumb is stung!

just the closing end of the cage momentarily to encourage the bees within to head for the light at the opposite end. You don't want to guillotine or trap any part of a bee as you close the cage, particularly not the queen!

The picking of workers is more daunting than picking the queen, because you fully expect to get stung. I routinely fill cages in this manner and it is extremely rare that I get stung, even on the thumb covering the slot. If this happens, remember that the important aspect is not the sting in your thumb but the fate of the queen in the cage. Best not to include the worker who has stung, since she will likely be fatally damaged.

Mated queens are the reward for our mating nuc endeavours. Take pride in each one, and introduce them onwards with care. There are many scenarios for introducing and making use of a young mated queen, and to describe them all would be beyond the scope of this book. However, one point I would like to emphasise is in relation to the attending workers within the cage - popular wisdom has it that they must be removed from the cage prior to introduction, or they will panic and ball the queen.

Our experience (and that of several large-scale queen-raisers with whom I have spoken) is that this is an extremely rare occurrence, and is more likely due to an un-receptive colony than to regicide by her own attendant workers. There appears to be far more chance of losing or damaging the queen whilst removing the attending workers, particularly with some of the faff that is earnestly advised regarding clear plastic bags and such like. This popular (but misguided) wisdom of having to remove the attendant workers appears to have arisen when importation rules required that the workers accompanying queens were separated before introduction and sent to the National Bee Unit for disease checks. When the requirement for this testing ceased, the imperative to remove the workers persisted, albeit under a different logic of supposed risk of balling.

We would always recommend that a caged queen is introduced with accompanying workers. Intuitively this would appear to have the benefit that rather than just a solitary queen, there are half a dozen bees in the cage now all carrying and transferring the queen's pheromones, aiding and speeding the acceptance of this new queen amongst the receiving colony. This retention of workers is, however, not a guarantee of successful introduction under all circumstances. It certainly is no substitute for staged introduction via a nucleus colony into a large or difficult colony, or where the new queen differs significantly in lineage or parentage from the recipient colony.

Using Apideas

4.4.4 Holding caged queens for short periods

Caged queens (with workers) can be held in their own Apideas for a few hours or indeed overnight, assuming that you have used an introduction cage of similar dimensions to the Swienty one. There are two ways to achieve this, each with its pros and cons.

Firstly, note the two rectangular cut-outs in the underside of the Apidea roof. The larger cut-out sits over the feeder in normal orientation, and should comfortably accommodate most plastic introduction cages. With the crownboard still in place but its flap folded open, place the queen cage on the crownboard over the feeder and replace the roof. The beespace channels in the underside of the roof will allow workers to access the queen cage.

Alternatively, lift the entrance slider right to the top, and pin or support it to prevent it from sliding back down. Remove the roof and crownboard, then slide out the large red grille. The raised entrance slider keeps the mini-nuc bee tight, but the removal of the grille creates a useful

Queen cage lodged at front

Slide the entrance slider to the top and remove the red grille to make a niche for a caged queen. This gives plenty of access for the workers, but removes almost all of the Apidea's ventilation.

4 Management

Maintaining a caged queen

A cage containing the queen and some workers from this Apidea is held overnight above the crownboard, under the larger of the rectangular roof indentations. Ensure the crownboard flap remains open to permit access by workers from the colony below.

shelf at the front of the hive, on which a plastic queen cage can be rested. Slip the now-surplus grille between the crownboard and roof, or between the Apidea floor and table, and it will be retained securely until needed again.

Both methods will give success. The former requires virtually no disturbance, but may give concern over the ease of access to the queen and (if the weather is changeable) less potential for the queen to share the colony's warmth. The latter is a quick rearrangement of the front of the Apidea, and gives very good access to and warmth for the queen cage, but greatly reduces the ventilation for the Apidea, which may be a concern on hotter days.

Using Apideas

4.4.5 Queen re-introduction

Under some circumstances, the queens that you have just removed from Apideas turn out to be not yet needed elsewhere. Perhaps you were planning to make up a certain number of nucs today, or move a certain number of laying queens onwards, but found that the donor colonies do not have quite as much brood or as many bees as you anticipated. Alternatively, somebody was going to collect a queen today but has now phoned to cancel or postpone.

In these circumstances, you realise the value of having written the mini-nuc number on the introduction cage when the queen was taken out - she can be returned to the colony that is familiar with her. They will of course have realised that they were queenless after 20 minutes or so. It is more 'normal' for a lost queen to reappear in her own colony, than for a recently queenless colony to be surprised by the arrival of an unfamiliar mature queen. Still, that caged queen is precious, so do not simply release her back into her own colony, which may have been queenless for some hours and may already be working on emergency queen cells. Allow time for familiarisation before releasing.

The simplest approach is to open the Apidea, remove the crownboard, and rest the caged queen over the frame top bars. After 3-5 minutes, note the behaviour of the workers who have come to inspect the queen cage.

The workers should be consistently interested, focused, and performing trophallaxis with the bees within the cage, in which case you should be safe to slide open the cage and let the queen re-join her colony. Test your smoker

Queenlessness test

A colony responds gently and enthusiastically to a caged laying queen placed over the frames of the brood box, indicating that it is queenless.

beforehand to ensure a rich puff of smoke is instantly available should any transient aggression be apparent.

Alternatively, if the workers are behaving aggressively towards the cage or its occupants, this demonstrates that the colony is not receptive to this queen. Check your cage and mini-nuc numbers to ensure you really are returning the queen to her own colony! It is better to introduce this queen to a different queenless colony than risk returning her to a colony when she is clearly unwelcome, even if you are sure it is her original colony.

This technique can be used as a quick queenlessness test for any colony. Cage a mature, laying queen from any other colony in the apiary, then rest this cage over the brood top bars of the suspect colony. The response of the interested workers after 5 minutes is usually one of:

Gentle sustained interest: queenless colony, receptive to queen introduction;

Aggression: probably either already queenright or advanced laying workers - inspect again;

No interest: no clear indication of queen status or the caged queen is resting too far away from the workers.

The only definite result is the first: gentle but sustained interest. Once you have a result, return the caged queen promptly to her own colony - they will hardly have missed her. Another myth is that she will have picked up a foreign colony scent in this time - she won't have been tainted during this short interlude, and will be welcomed back.

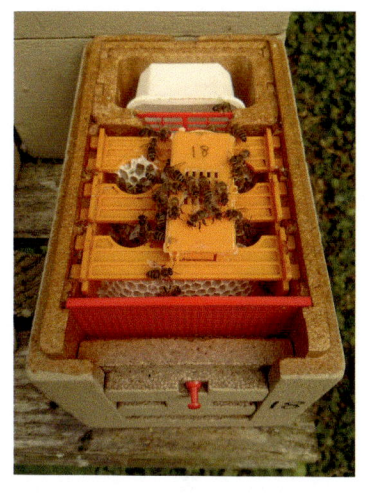

Queen re-introduction

This queen was caged but not used, so is being returned to her original Apidea after an absence of several hours. Workers are inspecting the cage calmly and with interest after only a minute ...

... and just five minutes later she has been released and is calmly accepted on the comb.

4.5 Recycle or close down?

Each time we have a laying queen present in a mini-nuc, we need to make a conscious decision as to whether the mini-nuc should recycled by introducing another ripe queen cell, or whether it is time to close this mini-nuc down. As long as there continue to be ripe queen cells coming ready from your queen raising activity, and the mini-nuc appears populous and healthy, recycling it would be the likely choice and is described in Chapter 5, *Recycling*.

The preferred method for closing down is to unite the mini-nuc over an established colony allowing the adult bees and any remaining brood time to join the colony. If the mini-nuc is queenright when closed down by uniting, it becomes a very effective method of re-queening a larger, queenless, colony. This is described in Chapter 6, *Closing down*.

4 Management

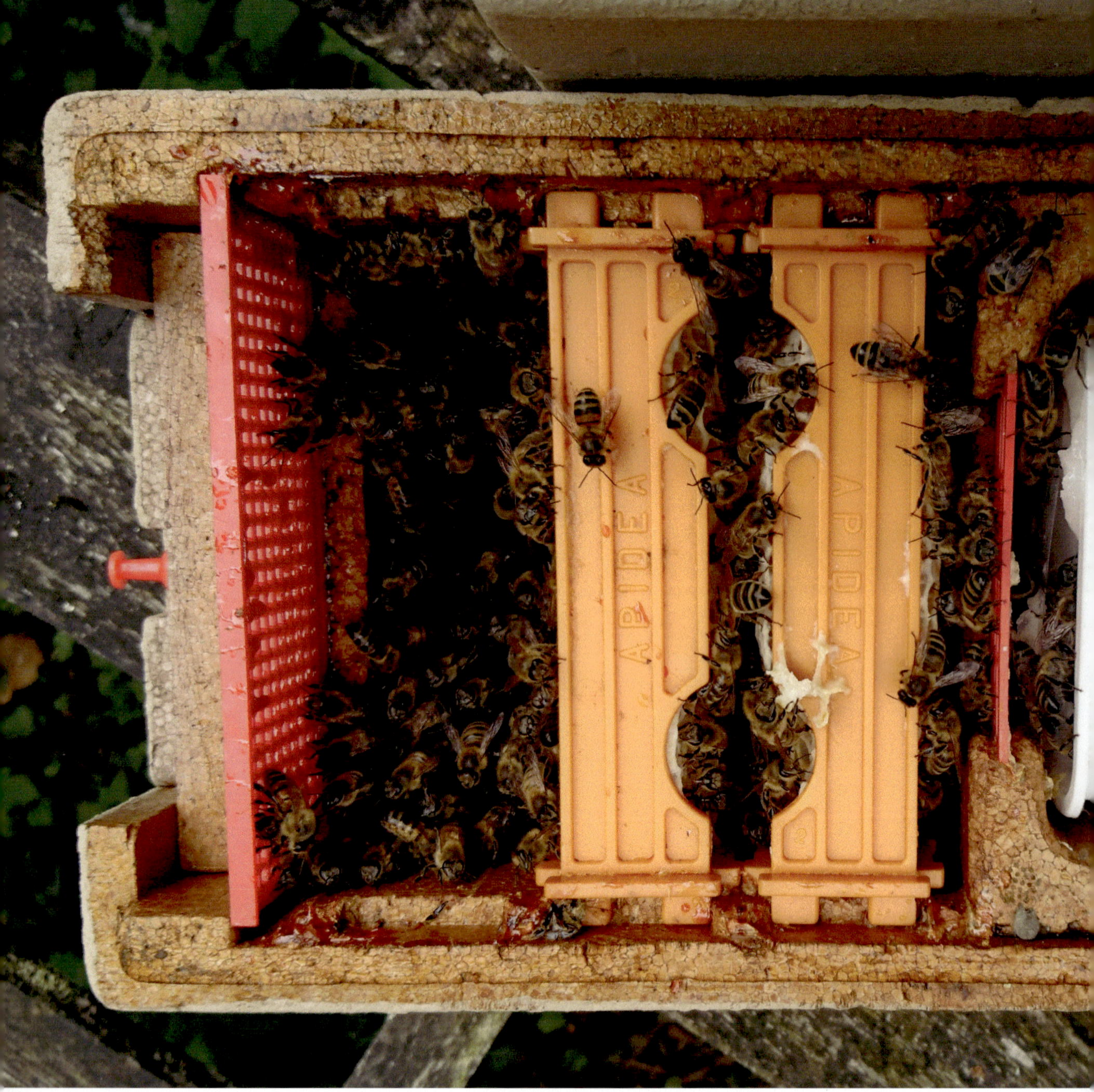
APIDEA
APIDEA

5 Recycling

Recycling occurs when a mini-nuc has had a mated queen removed, and then has another ripe queen cell introduced. The process of emergence, mating, and laying then repeats, using the already-established colony in the mini-nuc.

Whilst an Apidea might repay its initial purchase price many times over by simply providing one mated queen per season, it is through recycling that the true utility (and much of the pleasure) of managing these mating nucs becomes apparent.

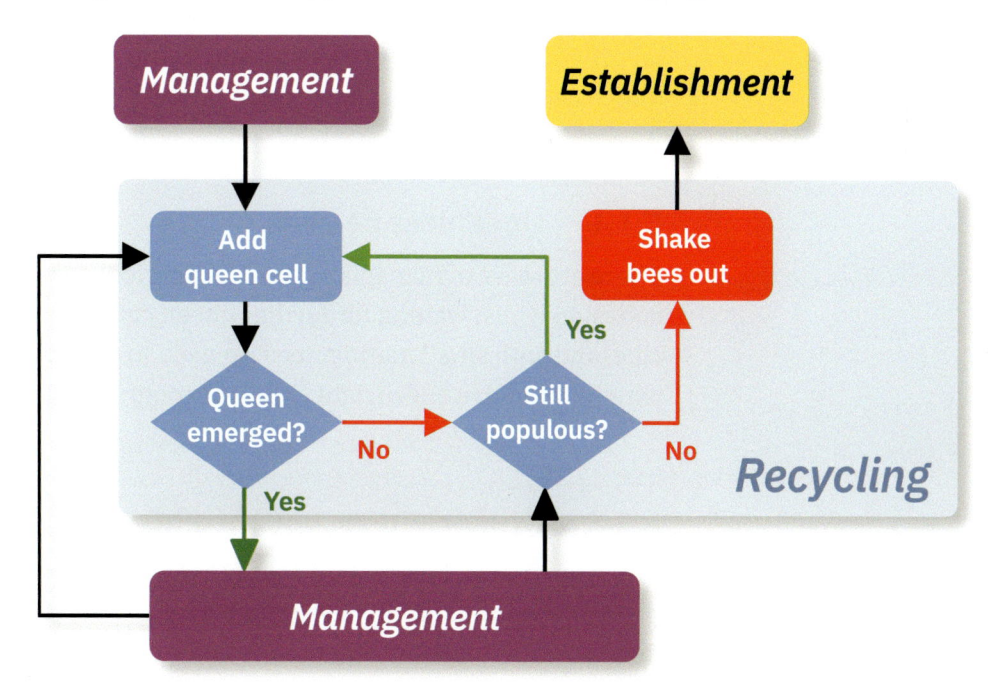

For me the 'normal' condition of a mini-nuc is not during the **establishment** phase, but as a populous and sustainable small colony, alternating between **management** and **recycling** stages. It is a pleasure to follow the progress of these little colonies through late spring and summer, and indeed they take on a degree of familiarity and become more than just a number.

For recycling to work, we must have a regular source of queen cells, and of course a regular destination for mated queens. This is essentially provided by a queen-raising pipeline operating on a 'little and often' batch basis.

5.1   Approach

Assuming that the first queen emerged and mated successfully, and that the mini-nuc retained most of its adult population, you will have a cohesive little colony with stores and brood in all stages. The brood laid by the first queen will develop, emerge, and bolster the ageing adult population even whilst the second queen is emerging and taking mating flights. This actually feels like a far better environment in which to entrust one of your precious ripe queen cells, than the establishment phase!

5.1.1   Queenless periods

There are ways of managing queenless periods to retain cohesion whilst waiting for further queen cells to come ripe, and with small mating nucs we need to consider whether they are queenright and / or broodright.

5.1.2   Broodright vs. queenright

Two principal factors make a colony cohesive: queen pheromones, and brood pheromone. Beekeepers are very familiar with the effect that the presence of a queen has on her colony, the terms **queenright** and **queenless**, and the implications (both short-term and long-term) of these two conditions. We are also aware of the change in temperament in a queenless colony, the breakdown of cohesion that starts to take place, and ultimately the appearance of laying workers. What is less generally understood is the parallel importance of brood pheromone to colony cohesion, particularly in the absence of a laying queen, such as happens when recycling Apideas.

If we are to maintain and manage our Apideas to each mate more than one queen in a season, we need to also consider the concept of **broodright** and **broodless** colonies. By ensuring that young brood is present, we can maintain cohesion for the period between the removal of a mated queen and the introduction of a ripe queen cell, even if there is a week or more between these events. Brood can be transferred in from another Apidea if necessary. This allows us to readily maintain a buffer state that can keep mini-nucs usable despite irregularities or mishaps in the queen cell supply.

Brood has a finite time before it emerges, and the supply

	Broodright	Broodless
Queenright	Ideal cohesion	Cohesive
Queenless	Cohesive	Laying workers developing

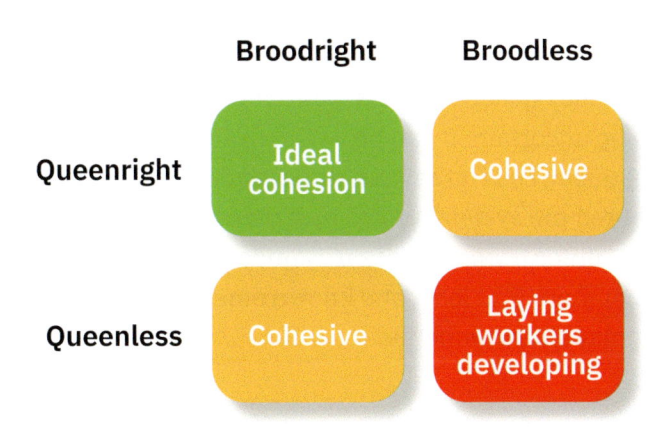

Queenright / broodright

Either condition on its own can keep a colony cohesive and defer the development of laying workers. Once a colony is queenless *and* broodless, it is only a matter of weeks before laying workers become apparent.

of brood pheromone is most abundant at the open brood stage. It is certainly not advisable to leave Apideas queenless for more than a fortnight - populations can quickly dwindle, with workers expiring or drifting away to queenright mini-nucs or hives nearby. Laying workers will become apparent within 2-3 weeks of the emergence of the last of the brood in a queenless colony, and at this point the colony ceases to function reliably as a mating nuc: shake out, clean, and re-establish from scratch.

The table above summarises the effects of managing queen and brood presence on colony cohesion. This is no different for a mini mating nuc or a full size colony.

5.1.3   Emergency queen cells

In a colony as small as an Apidea, the absence of the queen will be common knowledge almost immediately. Quite naturally, a queenless but broodright colony will look to make emergency queen cells from any suitable brood, whether its own or that donated to keep it broodright. This is a positive step and helps to further sustain a cohesive state, but emergency queen cells should be considered as sacrificial.

Because of the variable laying date of the larvae in emergency queen cells, the queen emergence date will also be uncertain. It can be useful to allow colonies to hold 'own queen cells' at certain times, and indeed in our coloured pin system we use blue pins to indicate this. These differ from an ordinarily queenless colony (red pin) in that there is at least one known emergency queen cell that may shortly emerge.

Whether mini-nucs can sufficiently feed emergency queen cells to result in good quality queens is the subject for a different discussion (the answer can still be 'yes', by the way) but in this instance we must principally question the parentage and performance of an emergency queen. She will be the daughter of the queen just mated in that mini-nuc, and hence the grand-daughter of the queen that we selected to breed from this season.

The variability of one-the-wing mating means that even when queen mating is going to plan from good stocks in a location blessed with good drones, we do not produce uniformly superior queens. Rather we raise a group of queens, most of whom we expect to perform above the average, with some being exceptional, some being disappointments.

The characteristics of an emergency queen's eventual colony will result from not only her character and matings, but her mother's character and matings. Remember that at this stage we don't even know yet how her mother is going to perform, or indeed whether her mother would be a queen we would choose to raise from.

The performance and pedigree of the Apidea-raised emergency queens will thus be more variable and less reliable than we might want. This is not to say that emergency queen cells should be knocked down immediately; their presence is part of a cohesive but queenless colony. They need to be managed consciously and in a timely fashion, ensuring that they are destroyed and ripe queen cells are substituted before the emergency queens can emerge.

5.2 Managing population size

5.2.1 Brood balancing

As mentioned earlier, the ideal is to keep a mini-nuc both queenright and broodright. However, should a mini-nuc experience a failure of queen emergence, or a queen lost on her mating flights, then the adult population of that mini-nuc will be steadily declining due to advancing age, with no replenishment via developing and emerging brood.

Part of the ongoing management therefore will be to take frames containing brood from congested queenright mini-nucs and give them to such queenless mini-nucs, ideally returning empty combs in exchange to the congested colony. This provides a very useful change in brood population for both colonies: one is boosted and given a supply of brood pheromone, the other is relieved of congestion and given brood-raising space.

I like to move frames of young, open brood into queenless mini-nucs as these will retain a cohesive effect for longer than sealed brood would. This technique, when applied more generally within beekeeping, is known as 'brood balancing' and comes with considerable caveats regarding the spread of disease. However, in the specific case of mini-nucs, this may be less of a concern if they were stocked from a common healthy source.

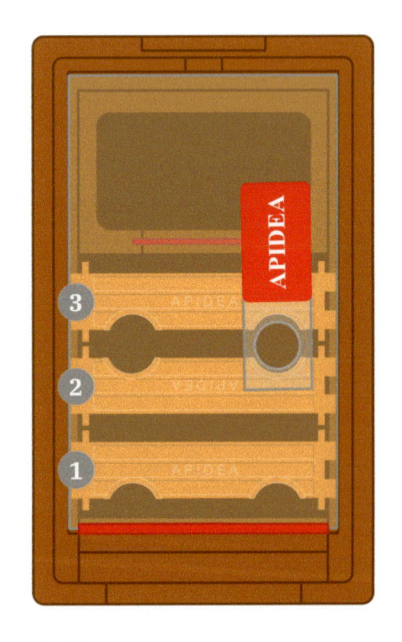

Egg laying by a newly-mated queen generally commences on frame 3 (closest to the feeder) in a standard Apidea configuration. If you make it a rule to introduce brood from another colony into frame position 2, then at subsequent inspections finding brood only on frame 2, with no eggs or brood on frame 3, should serve as an indicator or reminder that this was donated brood. You don't want to mistake introduced brood and clip and mark a queen who has not yet come into lay.

5.2.2 Bolstering by exchange

Similar to brood balancing, the adult bee populations can be balanced by exchanging a strong and a weak mini-nuc at dusk. Provided neither mini-nuc contains a queen taking mating flights, and both are visually identical, the subsequent redistribution of foragers back to their familiar locations is usually a harmless process.

If a queen in either mini-nuc is taking mating flights, such an exchange would induce her to return through habit to the wrong mini-nuc. At best she will be accepted into a queenless mini-nuc (but play havoc with your record keeping!), at worst she will enter confidently but be balled as a foreign queen in an already queenright mini-nuc.

Exchange can be quite a blunt instrument for colonies as small as Apideas when the flying workers return to their habitual spot. Instead of resulting in two reasonably evenly-populated mini-nucs, it may result in a simple exchange of strength: the weak mini-nuc becomes strong and the strong mini-nuc becomes weak, leaving you no further forwards. This is especially likely when one mini-nuc contains a laying queen and the other does not - workers from both mini-nucs gravitate towards the queenright colony. It is best to exchange mini-nucs which are both in the same state.

Using Apideas

Adding adult bees at entrance

Wetted queenless bees are scooped or shaken at the entrance of a weak Apidea, entering meekly and bolstering the population.

5.2.3 Bolstering with adult bees

Should the adult population of a mini-nuc dwindle over time, particularly when queenless, an alternative technique to exchanging the positions of mini-nucs is to bolster any weak mini-nucs directly with additional workers. Ensure first that the weak mini-nuc is broodright, giving a frame of brood if necessary, as this will enhance cohesion and retention as additional workers are assimilated.

The process is very similar to that of making up the mini-nucs in the first place: collect young workers from a healthy colony, and confine them - queenless - in the dark for at least 24 hours. These bees can be taken to the mating apiary, sprayed lightly with water or weak syrup to subdue them, then scooped out and deposited in front of weak mini-nucs. After a brief period of confusion, they will enter the nearby mini-nuc steadily and submissively.

Adding adult bees at entrance

Wetted queenless workers are shaken in front of several Apideas early one morning in order to bolster their populations.

5.2.4 Bolstering with emerging brood

Another approach would be to provide the weak Apidea with a frame of pre-emergent brood taken from a stronger Apidea. Such brood can be identified by the greyish hue that the brood cappings take on when the bees within develop their final colouring during the day prior to emergence. Usually you also see a number of bees chewing their way out, and ragged vacated cells indicating recent emergence.

This technique is not limited to the management of Apideas, but it relies on having emerging brood in Apidea frames at the time that it is needed. It can thus be useful to maintain a number of queenright Apideas extended with upper brood boxes to act as brood donors, either for generally bolstering colonies or to keep queenless colonies broodright. Managing such extended Apideas is discussed in Chapter 8, *Advanced Techniques*.

Emerging brood colour

Sealed brood that is about to emerge takes on a greyish hue as the bees within develop their final colouring. This provides an almost immediate source of emerging adults, suitable for bolstering any weak colony.

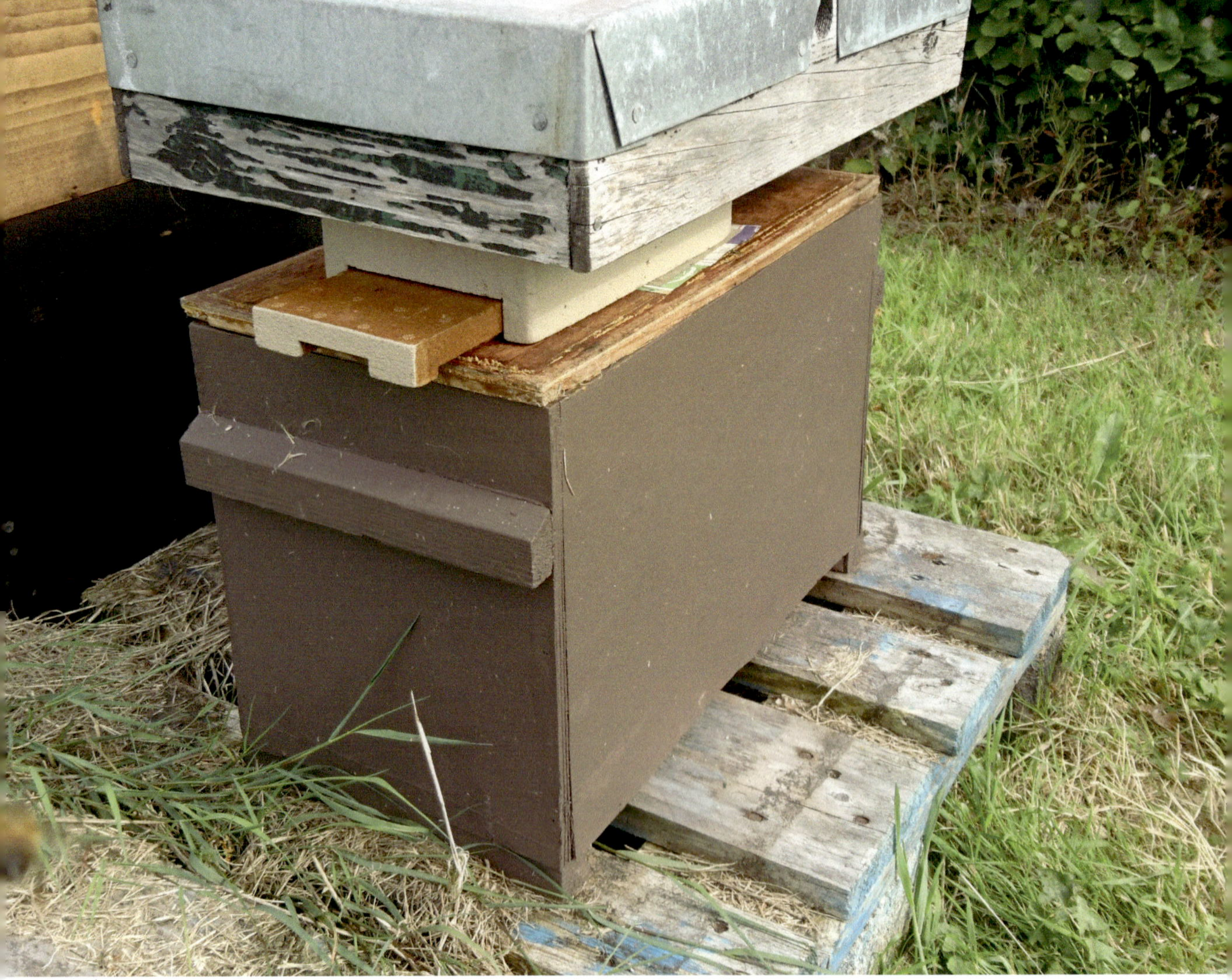

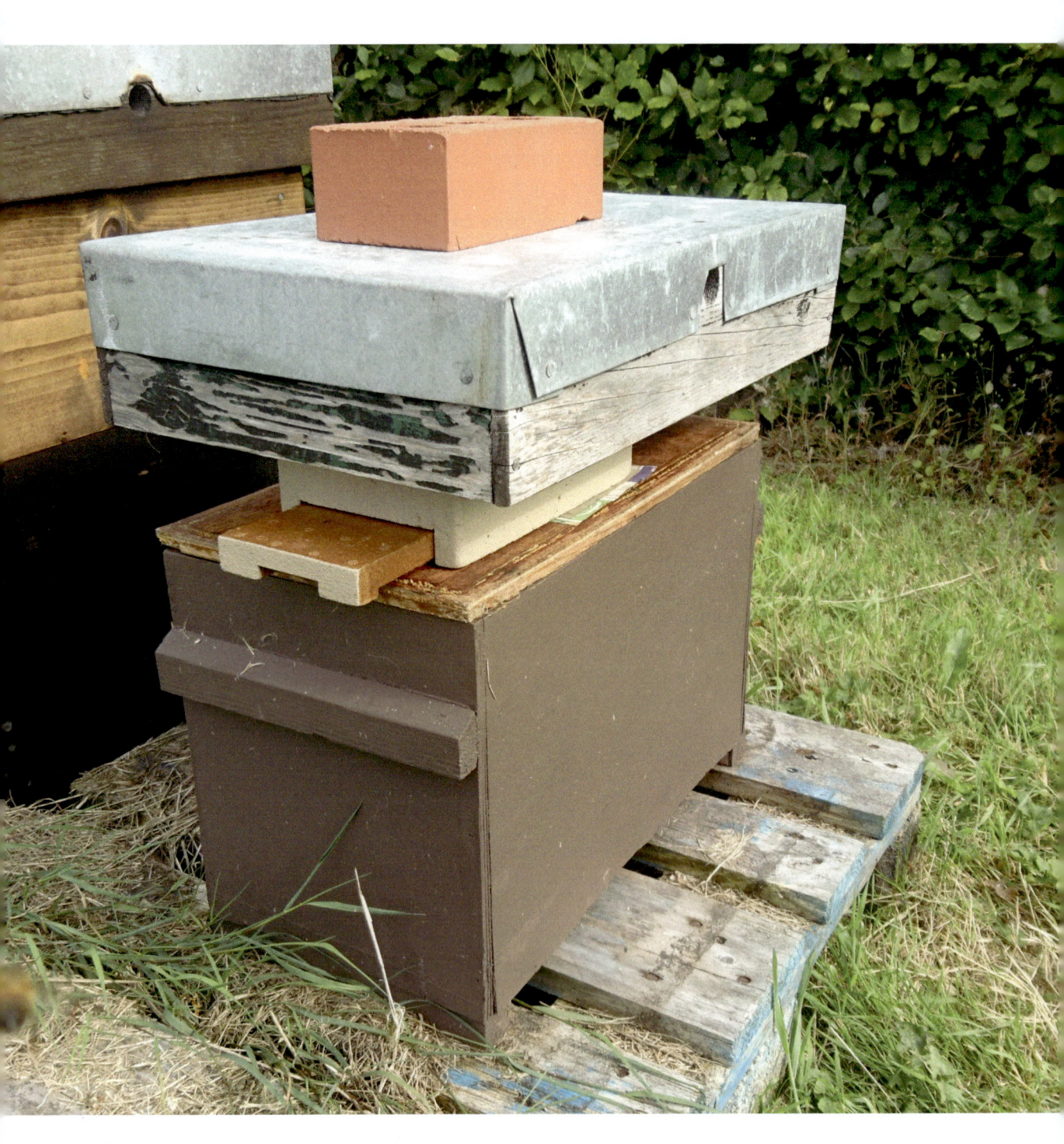

6 Closing down

In closing down we unite an Apidea onto another colony, usually to re-queen that colony, allowing time for any remaining brood to emerge. This makes for a sympathetic end for the little mating colony, and is a very effective method of queen introduction to a larger colony

As you reach the end of your queen raising for the season, you will need to plan to close down your mini-nucs in a positive and constructive fashion. Do not simply allow them to dwindle in a queenless state once the last mated queen has been removed - they deserve better than that.

In late summer, you may find that your hand is forced. Wasps can strip out a small mini-nuc in a day, and will move to the next smallest one, and then the next one, unless aggressively trapped. Your mini-nucs may rapidly become unsustainable in late July or early August as wasp robbing reaches its peak.

The cleanest close-down is simply to unite a queenright mini-nuc over a queenless colony. Workers, brood, and indeed stores from the mini-nuc can be usefully incorporated into the combined colony, a far more sympathetic fate than the alternatives. It is by far my preferred close-down technique.

However, closing down should not be viewed solely as an end-of-season activity. Uniting can be used at any point in the mating season as a form of supercharged queen introduction. Whilst it closes down an active mini-nuc mid-season, the whole mini-nuc population act as ambassadors for their queen, being much more persuasive than when a queen is introduced by a cage. The chances of successful acceptance of the new queen are greatly enhanced.

In most cases it is unrealistic to consider retaining mini-nucs over the winter to hold spare mated queens. Whilst it is indeed possible to overwinter them (see Chapter 8, *Advanced Techniques*) it is not reliable, with mini-nucs easily lost to starvation. There is much more security in uniting a

Using Apideas

Closing down by uniting

A classic newspaper unite, adapted by the addition of the empty super to securely accommodate the different hive patterns. The entrance slider of the Apidea is closed, but its floor has been slid out a couple of inches to provide access from below through the paper.

queenright Apidea onto a larger colony for overwintering a spare queen - even when uniting to a late-season nuc that will winter in a poly hive.

6.1 Equipment and preparation

Whether mid-season or late-season, queenless or queenright, the principle of uniting a mini-nuc onto a larger colony is the same: basically a newspaper unite.

Ensure that the mini-nuc has been closed (i.e. no flying permitted) before the day of the unite. Close the mini-nuc up the night before, even if it's on the same site – ensuring the maximum number of attendant workers are present to represent the queen during the unite. If the target colony is queenright and your intention is to re-queen it with the mini-nuc, remove the target colony's queen before proceeding with the unite.

Arrange for an empty container to surround the mini-nuc, to keep the process weather-proof and robber-proof. A National super is just too shallow to accommodate an Apidea, but you can add sufficient space by using an eke in conjunction with a super. Alternatively, an empty Commercial super fits just right, and an empty National or Commercial brood box provides more than enough space.

If you are uniting to a nucleus, ideally get hold of an upper brood box for that nuc pattern to contain the mini-nuc. Alternatively, if you have nuc boxes with integral floors, invert an empty spare nuc box over the united combination as an improvised upper container and roof. A brick will weigh it down, and if it's the sort with an integral mesh floor arrange for a temporary cover (such as a sheet of polythene) to shed the rain. The photo at the start of this chapter shows yet another simple approach if you have proper crown boards for your nuc hives - the Apidea is united over the crownboard and a brick holds the roof on top. Shower proof and bee tight, but definitely a fair-weather option!

If the target colony is particularly populous, or you are uniting bees of differing races, consider a staged unite:

mini-nuc –> nucleus –> target colony

Some years ago we acquired some Danish Buckfasts to trial alongside our loosely Devon Buckfast stocks, and found them particularly difficult to introduce. Colonies were still behaving aggressively towards the new queens even after four days of sealed-cage introduction (where the queen cage is introduced with the flap kept closed to check for acceptance before mixing can take place – a useful technique when changing race or introducing expensive queens). Noting this obvious sign of impending rejection, we made up queenless Apideas, introduced the imported queens into these during 3 days confined in the dark. Next, we made queenless nucs from the target colonies, then united the Apideas onto these nucs. Finally, we re-united the now-queenright nucs back with their just-dequeened parent colonies. A bit of a performance, but logical as a 'belt and braces' safe route to queen introduction through progressively larger but queenless target populations, and completely successful.

Using Apideas

6.2 The unite

Place a sheet of newspaper over the target colony, using the corner of a hive tool to prick 3-4 points in the paper directly under where the front of the mini-nuc will sit. Place the empty box over the newspaper to hold it in place. Take the closed mini-nuc and, ensuring that the entrance remains closed, place it over the pricked newspaper, pulling the floor slide out by 2-3 inches as you do so, to the extent of the space within the surrounding box. With the Apidea (and faithful copies) this still leaves the mini-nuc bee tight, with the only route out being through the newspaper.

If there are no supers, close the hive up with crownboard and roof. If supers need to be returned, just arrange a sandwich unite with an additional sheet of newspaper above the Apidea but under the supers, supported by a queen excluder, and let them sort themselves out.

Access through newspaper

Within an hour, a number of small holes will have been chewed through the paper, and the bees from both sides will have calmly mixed.

6.3 Follow-up

Under normal circumstances, contact and mixing of bees is achieved through newspaper in about an hour. Whilst you could check on the day after uniting to ensure the newspaper has been breached, the real indicator of success is that eggs are laid in the target colony – which should be visible within 2-5 days if all went to plan.

The mini-nuc can be removed after a few days, once the queen is laying in the target colony below, or can remain in place for three weeks until any remaining brood in mini-nuc frames has emerged. The latter approach is clearly most sympathetic, and even a couple of hundred extra young bees are a bonus to the target colony.

You may find, particularly late in the season or when the target colony itself is weak, that the queen is reluctant to leave the cosy confines of the polystyrene mini-nuc even a week after uniting. She stays in the Apidea, despite having little or no room for laying. Provided the newspaper has been breached, simply pick the queen from amongst the mini-nuc frames and deposit her on the top bars of the frames in the target colony below. Once she has moved down, cover the target colony with a queen excluder and then place the mini-nuc and surrounding box above that queen excluder. The workers still have access to attend to the brood and consume any remaining stores in the mini-nuc, but the queen cannot return and must find laying space in the box below.

If the target colony is a nucleus for which you do not have an appropriately-sized queen excluder, cut up a plastic or punched zinc queen excluder into 6" squares to place under the open floor gap of Apideas.

Queen excluder square

Here a square cut from a standard queen excluder sheet has been placed under the Apidea after a successful unite, in order to retain the queen in the nucleus hive below.

This technique works even without a crown board in place (i.e. directly over frames) since the opening in the floor of the Apidea has a consistent flat boundary on all sides, preventing any access except through the queen exlcuder.

Using Apideas

Uniting over a full-size hive

Here an Apidea is to be united over a populous colony. A crown board is being used to prevent access into the void around the Apidea to avoid wild comb drawing.

Make a few nicks in the paper with the corner of your hive tool above the feed hole of the crown board.

Place the Apidea with its floor slid open, so that the gap in the underside is aligned with the feed hole of the crownboard.

Here, a Commercial super has the height to comfortably enclose an Apidea whilst it is being united onto a National hive.

A successful unite, clearly showing how the Apidea floor gap, paper, and feed hole of the crown board were aligned.

Note that the exposed comb has been elongated - common when an Apidea is being retained over the target colony until all its brood has emerged.

6 Closing down

Too cosy upstairs?

Through its clear crownboard you can see that this Apidea has been bolstered to the point of overcrowding by bees from the main colony. This generally indicates that the queen has not gone down to lay in the full-size frames below.

The same united Apidea with the frames removed, and we find the queen still present in the cosy polystyrene attic.

The accepted queen is removed from the Apidea and placed in the brood box of the full-size hive below. A queen excluder added under the Apidea prevents her from returning to it, but allows workers to access any remaining brood and stores.

138

Using Apideas

Uniting over a nucleus hive

Ensure the entrance slider is closed and the floor is slid out by about two inches.

Wild comb drawing may be less of a risk with a smaller nucleus colony, so a crownboard may not be necessary under the Apidea.

An empty upper nuc box encloses the unite, keeping the colony weather-proof and secure from robbing.

This pattern of poly nuc uses a Miller-type feeder placed just under the roof; the accessible void around the Apidea retains access to the feeder by the nuc population.

Within an hour the bees will have united through small holes in the paper. Within a day or two they will have enlarged the holes greatly.

Here we used only enough newspaper to cover the opening on the underside of the Apidea. No more is needed.

6 Closing down

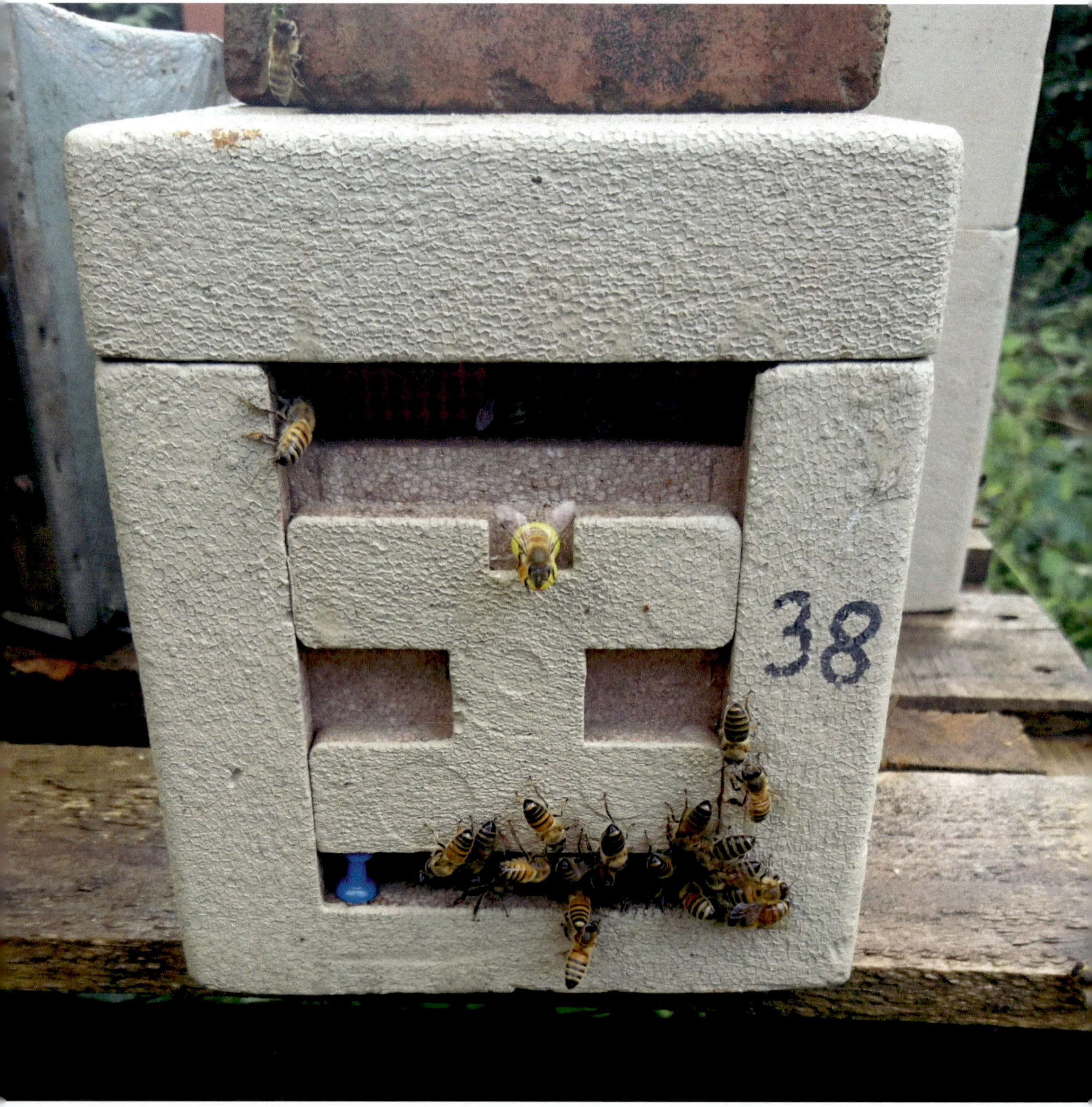
38

7 Reading Apideas

This chapter provides a visual guide to a number of conditions and situations encountered when managing Apideas and similar mini mating nucs.

Whilst teaching the National Diploma in Beekeeping's Advanced Course over many years, my father introduced the term **reading bees**. A beekeeper adept at this can look over a colony and make a reliable assessment of not only its past and current states, but also its likely future state. It is a skill reliant upon observation, knowledge, and experience.

So it is with mini-nucs. Due to the limited season and scope of management of these little colonies, the scenarios encountered are usually a subset of those experienced by full-size colonies. We would not expect to encounter supersedure or swarming, for example. Instead we are more likely to encounter starvation, dwindling or congestion. Foremost in our observation of the state of a mini-nuc is not simply whether it is queenright or queenless, but where precisely it is currently on the journey from ripe queen cell to mated queen.

Observation does not start when the first frame is pulled from the hive; it begins as we enter the apiary. How is the weather, the local forage, the state of flow? What is the general activity around the mini-nucs, and around other colonies that may be in the same apiary? As we move closer to the Apideas, do any show obvious signs of problems, through debris or pest damage? When lifting a roof off, what can we see through the crownboard before venturing further?

When looking at mating nuc combs (of any size or pattern), do remember that you may well be disturbing a flighty young queen who might readily take to the air, and perhaps be lost. Fight the urge to clear bees aside and peer into the combs, hoping to see eggs. Instead, check first for the queen and note if she is agitated or calm, and then either close up or go back through to check for eggs as a secondary task. Queens move around, brood stays put.

Using Apideas

143

7.1 Good population size

A well-populated Apidea will have bees covering both frames 2 & 3 (middle and closest to feeder), with those combs well drawn out.

1. **Well covered frames** - With good ambient light, a glance through the crownboard should give a fair indication of the colony size, although reflections can obscure your view; it is still clear here that the bees are well covering frames 2 & 3; and

2. **Taking the crownboard off** gives a better view, but of course some bees rise or disperse due to the disturbance. Now we have a clear view between the combs and into the feed cartridge to assess the number of bees present. The white pin indicates that a ripe queen cell was given at last inspection; the population size and cohesion suggests that she has emerged and has been accepted.

3. **This Apidea has mated its first queen** - She is laying and the colony is cohesive, despite the population having dwindled a little. Two well-drawn combs of brood and stores bode well. This colony is about the smallest you'd use for recycling - perhaps bolstering first with a frame of emerging brood, or by shaking additional workers in front.

4. **Recycled successfully** - By comparison with the previous photo, this Apidea has already been recycled successfully and a second or third queen is now laying. The colony is populous and thriving, having been bolstered by emerging brood from the previous queen's laying; its current queen has mated successfully and is laying well across combs 2 & 3.

Using Apideas

7.2 Population too small

The biggest hurdle with establishment lies in having the first queen cell fail to emerge. Some bees will disperse to other queenright mini-nucs, and most of the remaining workers will be camped in the feed compartment, consuming stores but showing little or no interest in comb drawing. Without brood or an emerged queen, there is nothing to give this colony cohesion. The tricky decision at this stage is whether they are still populous enough to risk giving them a second queen cell.

1. **A classic failed first queen cell emergence**, and unless many more bees are apparent once the crownboard has been lifted, it looks like many of the original workers have departed. I would not risk a second queen cell here; rather I would shake out the remaining bees and re-stock this Apidea from scratch before adding a queen cell.

2. **Another failed first queen cell emergence**, but this time the population is stronger and I would confidently try a second ripe queen cell in here. The difference is subtle, but here the feed compartment and the area between the feeder and frame 3 both appear to be well filled with workers, unlike in the previous photo.

3. **An angled shot of another failed emergence** shows how few bees remain and that there has been almost no attempt to draw any of the foundation strips. This colony is too small to risk another queen cell - again, shake out and re-stock.

Using Apideas

7.3 Failed queen cell emergence

It is rarely apparent why a queen cell failed to emerge. Opening such a cell gives little away: very often just an almost fully formed queen, much darkened - through late-stage development or through decay? Perhaps she was diseased, perhaps she was neglected by the mini-nuc population - but why?

In the absence of any meaningful clues, we simply accept such failures and go back round the cycle of either adding another queen cell if the Apidea remains populous, or shaking out and re-stocking from scratch.

1. **Camping in the feeder** - The queen cell of this newly-established Apidea failed to emerge. At first inspection after putting out, all the workers were massed in the feed compartment and ignoring the frames, a classic sign of failed emergence.

2. **No foundation drawing** - The same Apidea from a different angle shows that there has been virtually no drawing of the foundation strips during the initial 3 days of confinement.

3. **A failed queen cell may be darkened** upon investigation, whereas it was not noticeably darkened when it was given to the Apidea just a few days earlier. Is this black queen cell virus (BQCV)? There was no such discolouration apparent when the queen cell was removed from the queen raiser and placed in to the Apidea. There is surprisingly little information available regarding BQCV, and I am not aware of any definitive photos of afflicted queen cells.

4. **Opening the cell** shows a darkened, hairless, but apparently well-formed queen. The colouring of the dead queen is much darker and shinier than she would have been had she have survived to emergence. I suspect that the darkening of both the dead queen and her cell is due to decay and release of bodily fluids after death.

5. **The corpse is shrunken and dried** - Closer examination often shows that the wing buds have not enlarged on these failed queens, indicating that they did not die in the last 24 hours prior to emergence.

Using Apideas

149

7.4 Entrance activity

A glance across the entrances of the Apideas can tell you a lot about them before you start inspecting. Here are some of the common and less common entrance sights that I have been greeted with over the years.

1. **Normal entrance activity** - It is unusual to see more than half a dozen bees at the entrance of even a populous Apidea during foraging weather. Sometimes none are immediately apparent!

2. **After inspection** - the disruption of inspection results in more bees at and around the entrance, both in an enhanced state of guarding and those who took to the air returning. Fanning quickly subsides after the inspection has finished.

3. **Mating flight fanning** - the time stamp on this photo shows that I took it just after 2pm in late May - prime time for mating flights, weather permitting. Before any smoke or disturbance, these workers were out fanning *en masse* at their entrance, indicating that their queen was out on a mating flight.

4. **Overcrowding** - 1pm on a hot July afternoon, when temperatures hit 27°C in the shade in the mating apiary. Workers have moved outside this Apidea to ease thermoregulation within. These Apideas were in full sunlight with no shade, yet they neither absconded nor suffered any apparent long-term ill effects.

5. **Queen balling** - an early photo from when I learned the lesson about morning inspections: this was the scene when a mating queen returned to the wrong colony due to the disruption of my ill-timed inspection - 3:30 pm in early August!

6. **Eviction of premature queen** - occasionally a queen cell is damaged during manipulation of the queen raising colonies; in this case a young queen was pulled from a damaged cell a day before natural emergence and dropped in through the crownboard of a queenless Apidea. In most cases, this mobile but 'drowsy' young queen would have been accepted; in this instance, she was immediately and forcibly evicted, with this worker harassing her even when outside of the hive.

Using Apideas

7.5 Good combs

Good comb drawing and utilisation are a sign of successful mini-nucs.

1. **Honey, pollen, brood in all stages**. An ideal comb to give to a small or queenless Apidea to keep them broodright and provide a modest population boost. Pollen on the comb helps even a small colony maintain this brood; eggs and young larvae may become emergency queen cells if the recipient colony is queenless.

2. **A good full frame of brood** contains 150-200 occupied brood cells per side and ensures population continuity and growth in an established Apidea. Alternatively, such frames could be removed to relieve congestion in a strong colony and given to a modest colony as a population booster, provided the recipient has sufficient adult bees to cover the brood and keep it warm.

3. **A frame of honey and pollen stores**, typical of a frame from position 1 (closest to the entrance) in a populous established Apidea.

4. **A frame completely filled with honey**, typical of an upper or outer frame from a 5 frame or double-brood Apidea. This and the previous frame could be given to other Apideas to add stores, particularly 5-frame Apideas (which have no feeder).

5. **Used combs** after a full mating season in one repeatedly recycled Apidea. The darkening is evidence of repeated brood raising cycles, and it is clear that the top frame has probably spent most time in position 3 - the favoured position for brood raising. Notice also that the lower right frame has had comb drawn and well-used the 'wrong way round' due to my experimentation with different starter strip orientations. Do bees care about this?

6. **An emergency queen cell** can help keep a queenless Apidea in a more normal natural state until you have a ripe queen cell ready to give. A populous Apidea is capable of raising a well-fed emergency queen, but you are raising a daughter of an unproven queen - is this really what you wanted the Apidea for?

Using Apideas

7.6   Erratic first laying

When a queen first comes into lay, her egg placement and fertilisation may be erratic. Initially you might see a handful of cells with multiple eggs placed in them, amongst areas of more regular laying. Also, the individual egg placement may be a little off as she learns how and where to deposit eggs. With time, it may be apparent in the first sealed brood that there have been a small number of drone-in-worker incidents - eggs which were not appropriately fertilised.

In small quantities, neither of these are cause for concern, indeed at the first sighting of eggs you will begin searching through the Apidea to find and mark the young queen and may miss seeing any cells with multiple eggs. By the time brood is being sealed, it will be very apparent whether drone-in-worker is an occasional or regular problem.

Be suspicious of any queens which come into lay a week or so after prolonged bad weather during their mating period. Whilst they may lay well through the summer, these queens may become drone layers over the coming winter.

1. **Multiple eggs** - A small number of cells in this comb show multiple eggs, however the surrounding cells all have perfect single egg placements. This queen settled quickly into being a good layer.

2. **Drone in worker cells** - From a different Apidea, the first sealed brood of a young queen shows two raised drone-in-worker cell cappings. Again, this was just an early glitch and this queen too settled down into being a good layer.

Using Apideas

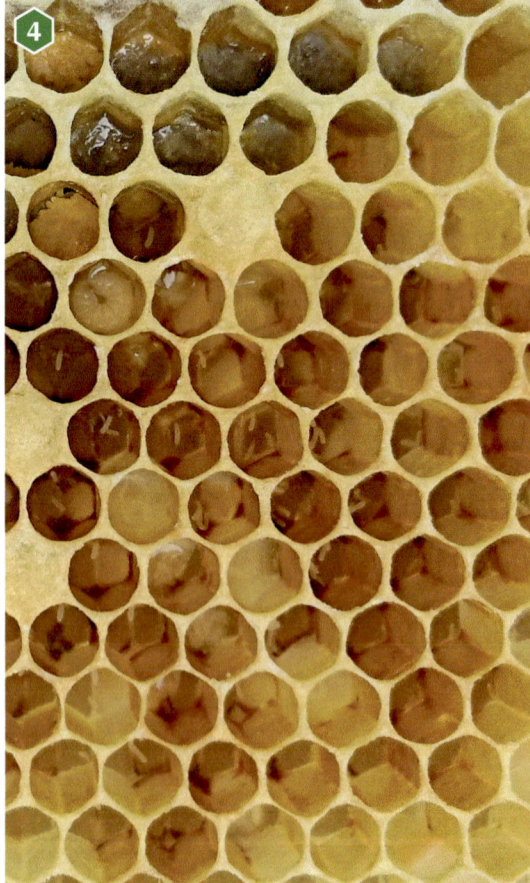

7.7 Constrained laying pattern

After any initial erratic laying, a young queen will settle down into regular egg laying. However, in the confined space of a mini-nuc she will rapidly run out of laying space and start to show multiple egg placements in the same cell which, at first glance, might be confused for laying workers. Essentially this is a constrained laying pattern, and finding the queen gives confidence that this is the cause of the multiple eggs. View this as a sign that this queen needs to be moved onwards imminently; you can buy time by swapping a laid-up brood frame out for empty drawn comb from another Apidea.

1. **Queen trapped in feeder** - The worst-case scenario of constrained laying is when the queen becomes trapped in the feeder compartment. Usually this happens because she runs up and over the top of the feeder whilst the crownboard is off for inspection, or she has been shaken or dropped from a frame into the feeder. Workers will attend to her and build comb as the feed is consumed, providing laying space which she enthusiastically fills, and fills again, with multiple egg placements. The queen is visible on the left of the white cut comb container tub.

2. **Multiple eggs** - Looking more closely into the comb in the same feed cartridge as previously pictured, the multiple egg placements are obvious, as is a cell just about centre that holds three tiny larvae. Workers will soon remove two of these to restore order.

3. **Multiple eggs** - In a different Apidea, constrained laying has led to multiple egg placements in some of these cells. The unmarked queen is just visible at the top right of the photo.

4. **Constrained queen or laying workers?** At the extreme, with very limited comb space and a vigorous queen, the egg placement really looks like that of laying workers. In this situation, either find the queen or establish that a queen is definitely not present. This colony was indeed queenright. Move her onwards quickly to avoid frustration!

Using Apideas

7.8 Laying workers

In the absence of a queen, and with a very small (or no) amount of brood, laying workers develop within 2-3 weeks. It is partly for this reason that an Apidea that fails to establish after receiving two successive ripe queen cells will be shaken out and restocked from scratch.

Laying workers will repeatedly lay into the same cell, and any brood that develops will be drone brood, necessitating enlarged 'domed' cell cappings on worker-sized cells. Whilst a newly-laying queen may lay erratically at first - producing occasional multiple egg placements, or the odd drone-in-worker - this is normally limited to a handful of cells unless there really is no other laying space in the mini-nuc. With laying workers, the problematic laying is widespread in such a small colony, usually coinciding with a lack of cohesion and a marked dwindling of the adult population.

The acid test, of course, is to carefully check all the bees in the mini-nuc to see if a queen is present - with such a small population this is relatively swift and straightforward.

It is pointless trying to 'save' a laying worker mini-nuc by, for example, repeatedly donating frames of open brood from other mini-nucs. It just isn't worth the time or effort. Shake them out and start again.

1. **Raised cappings** - Even before you lift out the frames, the extensive domed cappings of drone-in-worker brood raise concern.

2. **Multiple eggs** - The same comb as previously, viewed from a different angle and showing multiple egg placements.

3. **Multiple egg placements** are very apparent against the darker pollen cells on the opposite side of this comb.

4. **Shake them out** - This colony was still relatively populous, but worker laying was very pronounced across both of its combs of brood.

Using Apideas

7.9 Queens with deformed wing virus (DWV)

Raise enough queens and you will occasionally see one with deformed wings. Look closer, and you may see that her abdomen appears dented or damaged. With no wings, she cannot take mating flights. I see perhaps one of these a season; if more became apparent I would be concerned about varroa levels in the queen raising colonies.

Retaining a DWV queen in a mini-nuc could hold that colony in a more cohesive state (just like, say, an emergency queen cell) when you have a delay in queen cells coming ripe. It is common to see DWV queens become hairless after a week or two, leaving them looking dark and oily. Whilst a dark, oily, hairless appearance is one of the signs of Chronic Bee Paralysis Virus (CBPV), the fact that none of the workers in either the mating nuc or in the queen raising colony have this appearance suggests that it is not CBPV affecting solely the queen. I assume instead that the workers become steadily more aggressive towards a maturing queen who refuses to take mating flights, including frequent biting.

I have experimented with leaving DWV queens in Apideas to see how long they are tolerated for. After a fortnight they look very abused, after about three weeks they are gone. My conclusion is that it is cruel to prolong their suffering, so any DWV queens now go swiftly into alcohol to preserve them for our autumn dissection courses.

1. **DWV queens quickly become hairless**, in contrast to the workers in the mini-nuc. In addition to the crumpling through deformity, her wings show tattered edges due to biting by the workers.

2. **Disfigured by nibbling** - Closer examination of the queen seen in the first photo showed that she had been so badly bitten that she had lost two feet.

3. **Dents and bulges** indicate deformities in the development of the abdomen.

4. **Look closely** - At first glance, a good queen, but look closely and the lack of wings and dented abdomen become apparent. She was marked to ease removal as soon as a ripe queen cell could be introduced.

Using Apideas

161

7.10 Disease

Chalkbrood is generally the first disease problem to be seen in mini-nucs, being a disease of a virtually endemic pathogen (fungal spores) triggered by stress. Do not tolerate this, or any other disease signs.

Should any disease occur, the Apidea is closed up that evening and removed from the apiary, then placed in a domestic deep freeze for 48 hours to kill the colony. We do not simply shake the bees out, since they would disperse around the other Apideas and hives in the mating apiary, taking chalkbrood spores with them.

The combs are melted down, any remaining fondant securely disposed of, and all hive parts are scraped, washed, and then sterilised by submerging in a bleach solution. See the National Bee Unit's *FAQ 16 - Hive Cleaning and Sterilisation* for more details of recommended procedures for sterilising polystyrene and plastic hive equipment in general. I discuss how we clean Apideas in Chapter 10, *Maintenance*.

1. **Classic chalkbrood mummies** were seen in the combs and on the floor of this colony. Apideas had been made up from colonies not noted as chalkbrood susceptible, but the fungal spores are virtually endemic and infection is triggered by stress - such as a small colony struggling to maintain brood nest temperature.

2. **Scrape and scrub** - After freeze-killing the colony, the bees, combs and remaining feed were securely disposed of, and all hive parts were scraped and then soaked and scrubbed in a washing soda solution.

3. **Soak in bleach** - After the washing soda, hive parts were then sterilised by submerging in a bleach solution for 20 minutes, followed by rinsing in clean water.

Using Apideas

163

7.11 Starvation

Apideas need close monitoring of stores and regular feeding to sustain them in the British climate. Bear in mind that we are in the dry, warm south east corner of Devon, and still starvation is an ever-present risk. The feed cartridge should be checked at least weekly and replaced when it is a third full (or less); generally a full cartridge lasts for three weeks of our changeable spring-summer weather.

1. **Dead brood and adults ejected** - This was one of several Apideas moved into the nuc-raising apiary in the autumn, ready for closing down by uniting onto late nucs. Unfortunately we did not check the stores situation sufficiently; by our next visit it was clear that this Apidea was starving.

2. **No honey or pollen stores in the combs** in the above colony, and the feeder was empty. Despite these dire conditions, the queen was still laying well - this frame is full of eggs. Presumably she had been fed sufficiently by her colony until quite recently. This underlines how quickly a mini-nuc can run short of stores in a few days of poorer weather. This Apidea was swiftly united to the nuc below it, securing the future of the surviving queen, workers, and brood.

3. **The dead queen and a few dead workers** were found still clinging to the combs in another Apidea which had starved. An unnecessary loss - check feed.

4. **June gap starvation** - In June, this Apidea was caught at the point of starvation during a period of good weather but with little or no income. Awaiting recycling, it was queenless with a modest amount of predominantly sealed brood. Some workers were clinging to the combs, just able to move, others had dropped to the floor of the Apidea or were lying dormant at the entrance.

5. **Revived with syrup and sunshine** - The workers from the floor, entrance, and combs were shaken together into a plastic tub, lightly sprayed with a 1:1 syrup spray, and left loosely covered in the sunshine for ten minutes. Thus revived, they were returned to the Apidea - along with feed of course. They would probably not otherwise have survived the night - it was very fortunate that we arrived and checked them just in time.

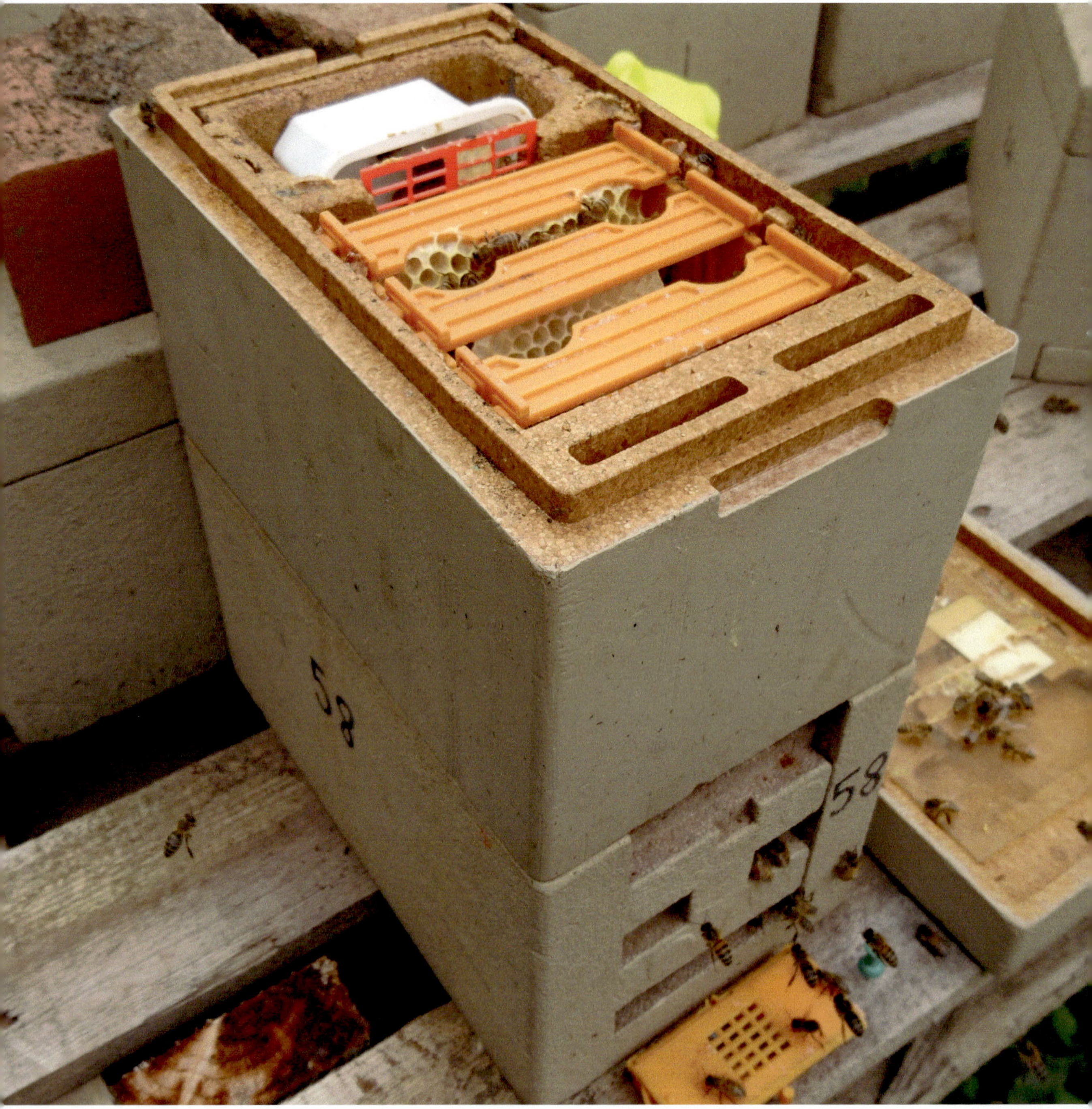
58
58

8 Advanced techniques

This chapter brings together some management techniques that provide interesting and useful extensions to the basic operation of mini-nucs.

It should be emphasised before we go any further that there is no particular need to expand mini-nucs beyond the basic 3 frames in order to perform their primary function.

It can, however, be useful at times to have larger, more populous Apideas that can act as donors of brood, stores, or drawn comb for smaller or more recently established units. Indeed it is possible to bring queenright Apideas through the winter to provide a pool of reserve queens to allow early replacements or expansion in spring.

It can also be interesting to allow a mini-nuc to expand, and to try different equipment combinations and observe how such a colony fares. In theory you could continue stacking up as many additional boxes as a colony can usefully occupy. The resulting tall narrow hive might need guy ropes for stability, and inspecting the many boxes and frames would require a high degree of patience and a very methodical approach!

Whilst this is all quite feasible, we are straying well beyond the intended function of the mini mating nuc, and the basic utility of being able to set one up at will with merely a cupful of bees.

8.1 3-frame to 5-frame

Following two consecutive successful mating cycles, a mini-nuc can become very populous with bees and brood. One simple expansion option is to take out the standard feeder and replace with two additional frames, giving a total of five frames in use.

Make this change whilst the mini-nuc has a newly-laying queen in place, and retain her there for around an additional week beyond the normal point of removal in order to have her lay up more brood in the additional frames.

My observation is that colonies in Apideas consistently arrange their brood away from

Using Apideas

the entrance, and stores towards the entrance. This may well be due to us habitually running the Apideas with their red ventilation grilles exposed, but it steers my approach when expanding to 5 frames: I move the brood backwards into the space vacated by the feeder and retain the stores at the entrance.

Two extra frames of part- or fully-drawn comb are then added between the brood and the stores. Even partially drawn comb is very much preferred to foundation strips, since without the feeder in place the colony will need a good nectar income in order to both sustain its immediate needs and draw additional comb. Separating the brood nest from the stores frame by two empty combs should not present a problem if the colony was sufficiently populous to have warranted the move to 5 frames.

A solid comb of honey must be retained as the primary food reserve in case of poor weather, since there is now no feeder and hence no fondant reserve. If this colony does not have such a frame (for instance if there is brood across

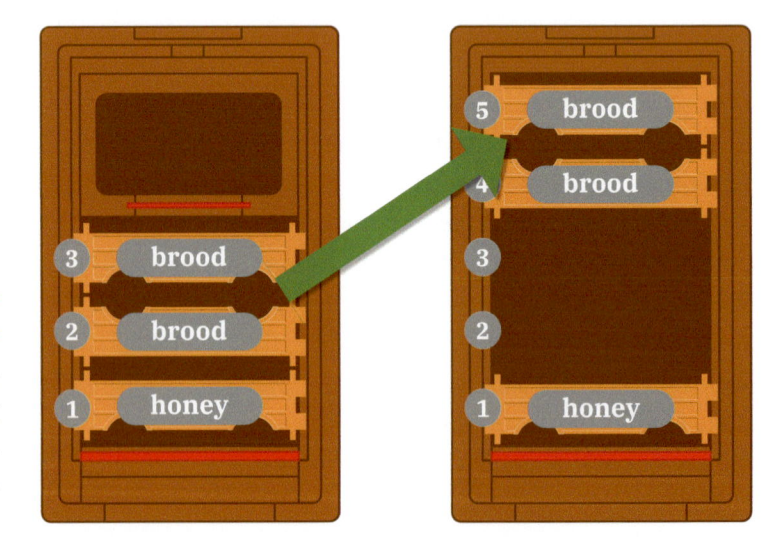

5-frame Apidea

You can remove the feeder to make space for two extra frames, allowing for a stronger mating nuc population.

Place brood away from the entrance

Transition to 5 frames by removing the feeder, moving the existing brood frames backwards, and adding frames between brood and stores.

all 3 frames, with only light peripheral stores) then take a full comb of honey stores from another mini-nuc that still has its feeder in place.

In experimenting, I have had equal success with either moving the existing brood frames to the back (positions 4 and 5) and placing the additional frames between the brood and the stores frame at the entrance, or indeed with moving the existing brood to positions 3 and 4, and placing the additional frames either side of the brood. This suggests that the precise arrangement of brood, stores, and space is not especially important to the bees during the expansion, and is more something of a beekeeper's preference. Whichever expansion route you choose, the frames can of course be reorganised at any subsequent inspection, based on how the colony utilises them over time.

When you next recycle a 5-frame Apidea, do first reorganise to ensure that there is generous amount of brood in frame positions 2 and 3. The introduced queen

Populous 5 frame Apidea

This colony has expanded to fill the 5 frames now available, a very encouraging progression. Do remember, though, that greater population means greater risk of starvation during poor weather.

Using Apideas

Queen cell placement in a 5 frame Apidea

Here a 5 frame Apidea is being recycled with a new queen cell. The queen cell is still placed between frames 2 and 3 by necessity of the location of the hole in the crownboard. Ensure that there is plenty of brood on frames 2 and 3 to retain attentive workers around the queen cell.

cell will be surrounded by brood, which will retain a good number of attentive workers around the queen cell.

In terms of regular management, the major difference with the 5-frame Apidea is its reliance on comb-stored honey and the inability to readily provide a reserve of fondant. If weather conditions are good, then a populous 5-frame Apidea should maintain ample stores in its frames. If the weather is poor or changeable, or during a period of sparse income (a June gap) then the 5-frame Apideas should be checked diligently for stores once a week. It is possible to pack the roof cavities with fondant and leave the crownboard flap open to facilitate access.

At each inspection, in addition to the usual checks for any mini-nuc, ask yourself the question *"Do they still need 5 frames?"*, and do not assume that the answer will be *"yes"* for the entirety of the season. It may be that after a failed mating cycle, or if a laying queen was moved on as soon as the first eggs were seen, the population will have declined naturally by not being replenished by sufficient emerging brood. At this point, revert in a planned fashion to a 3-frame layout with a feeder, rather than risking further decline, stress, and hunger.

To revert from 5 frames to 3, get all of the frames out, inverted on the roof, so that you can see what you have to work with. If the mini-nuc is queenright, either cage the queen temporarily for certainty, or ensure she is on one of two inverted frames placed close together on the roof and she should move comfortably to the shaded space between them. Choose the 3 frames that will stay with the colony - noting that this does not strictly need to include a solid frame of honey once the feeder is back in place.

Turn the empty mini-nuc body over and slide the floor out completely. Brush any remaining bees from the inner sidewalls at the rear, insert the empty feeder, then slide the floor back in, taking care not to crush any inquisitive workers. Add your three chosen frames, add a cartridge of fondant, and if you have caged your queen re-introduce her now. Shake any remaining bees from the two surplus frames back onto the top bars or at the entrance, and then close with crownboard and roof.

Reverting from 5 frames to 3

The population of this Apidea has declined from its peak a month earlier. It is being prepared for reverting to 3 frames so that a standard feeder can be added, although a spare feeder was not to hand during this inspection.

The combs have been rearranged to place the three chosen combs at the front. The two rear frames will be replaced by a feeder at the next inspection (as no spare feeders were to hand at this visit).

Using Apideas

8.2 Second brood box

A purpose-made upper box is available to extend any Apidea. Whilst we might equally term this a super or a brood box, in practice we are essentially just managing the colony over two boxes of the same depth, with brood and stores in both, so I consider it a double brood system.

Expanding a strong 3 frame Apidea onto a second brood box has a major advantage over progressing from 3 frames to 5 frames – the feeder is retained through the expansion. This gives a more immediately manageable reserve should the weather subsequently change, and the fondant feed assists greatly with drawing any foundation added.

The transition to a second brood box starts exactly as for the transition from three to five frames, i.e. populous and queenright, with the brood retained in the lower box. Move the feeder into the upper box, move the existing brood frames to the rear of the lower box. Add two frames, ideally of drawn comb, into the lower box, and foundation strips into the upper box.

As the colony expands into its larger home, the queen may readily lay into the upper frames once drawn, cocooned as they are in a small warm space above the existing brood nest. Retain the laying queen for longer than you would in a standard single-box Apidea, at least until there are three or four frames of brood in the lower box and one or two in the upper box.

Once all 8 combs are drawn and in use, you could of course then remove the feeder and add two further frames. In this 10-frame configuration, the optional upper

8-frame Apidea

With a second brood box in place, the colony expands the brood nest into the upper box. Here an 8-frame Apidea is being recycled with a ripe queen cell added between upper brood frames.

8 Advanced techniques

feeder will be needed if you wish to provide a buffer of fondant as insurance against periods of poor weather - a populous double-brood Apidea can get hungry very quickly.

When you recycle a double-brood Apidea, rearrange frames to ensure that there is open brood in positions 2 and 3 in the upper box - i.e where the queen cell will be suspended. Introduce the queen cell through the flap in the crownboard as usual and that open brood in upper frames 2 and 3 will retain an attentive cluster of workers around the queen cell, just as in a basic 3-frame single-box Apidea.

Whilst inspecting a double-brood Apidea, borrow a second roof (or carry a spare) so that you have one inverted roof on which to stand the upper box, plus another inverted roof on which to place your frames as you work through either the upper or lower box. Place the upper box at a slight diagonal across the inverted roof, and this will minimise the contact points (crushing points). It should be fairly obvious that if you are using pallet tables as I do,

Double brood inspection

The upper box is placed to the right on an additional inverted roof, whilst the lower box is inspected first. Frames are laid out on an upturned roof as for a single box Apidea, and both boxes are accessible at once so that frames can be freely rearranged into either box.

172

Workers clustering under upper brood box

Check under the upper box for clustering workers before placing it back over the lower box. A puff of smoke will send these bees up onto the frames and prevent them from being crushed, particularly under the feeder.

Condensation

The upper box has no ventilation grille of its own, so condensation can gather under the crownboard. This does not seem to be harmful, and indeed the condensate may be gathered by the bees to help liquefy fondant in the feeder.

placing the removed upper box straight onto the pallet invites all sorts of chaos with workers and queens ending up on the underside of the pallet timbers, perhaps clustering there or even dropping into the vegetation below the table. The extra roof avoids this - don't invite mishaps!

Do take care when re-assembling the boxes as workers will often cluster below the frames and feeder of the upper box whilst it is standing over an inverted roof. There is only a single beespace between the broad top bars of the frames in the lower box and the hard underside of the feeder in the upper box, so these clustering bees might easily be crushed. A puff of smoke and a short pause before re-assembly will allow these bees to disperse away from the feeder and upwards onto the frames – far better than crushing them. Do take further care not to crush bees between the stepped lower and upper box rims as they come together – judicious use of smoke should disperse them from here too.

8.3   Upper feeder

Another optional extension for the Apidea is the upper feeder, which fits as a shallow full-size feeder above an Apidea or an upper brood box. This allows for a greater amount of feed to be given to an extended and more populous Apidea in order to more rapidly draw combs and store feed within them.

There is no provision to limit the bees' access to the full feed tray, so unless you arrange a float or ladder mechanism, many bees will drown if you add syrup to the feeder. Despite their agility on the smooth inner polystyrene walls elsewhere within the Apidea, the polystyrene does not allow sufficient foothold for sodden bees to drag themselves out of the syrup in the feeder. Instead, fill the feeder with fondant and this can be safely consumed.

Given that the standard feeder compartment is free, so easy to use with cut comb container feed cartridges, and will sustain an Apidea through a fortnight of wet weather, I don't really see the need for these additional feeders.

Apidea upper feeder

Do not feed syrup unless you can arrange a float or ladder mechanism. The polystyrene walls do not give sufficient foothold for bees to climb out of the syrup. Fill the feeder with fondant instead.

8.4 Entrance queen includer

The Apidea comes with a queen includer for the entrance – this can be pinned on and operated as shown. The primary use of this entrance queen includer is to hold emerged virgin queens that are destined for instrumental insemination.

I hear of some beekeepers using this entrance queen includer to contain mated queens for long periods; if this is simply masking the problem of having nowhere yet to move mated queens onward to, then it is this 'onward' bottleneck that needs to be resolved, rather than imprisoning an increasingly frustrated laying queen within a mating nuc.

The German equipment supply company Heinrich Holtermann sell drone includers of a similar pattern to the standard queen includer, to keep any drones within the Apidea. If Apideas are to be transported to an isolated mating apiary, any drones included when Apideas are established will 'pollute' the mating apiary.

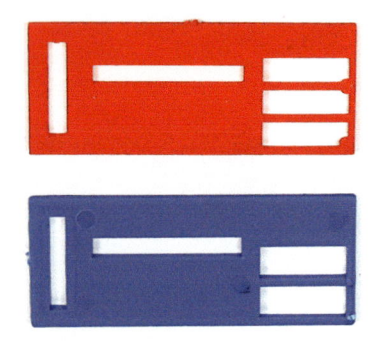

Entrance includers

At the top is the red queen includer supplied with each Apidea. It can be pinned across the entrance to retain a queen within the Apidea.

The blue piece is a drone includer: it allows queens and workers to pass but restrains any drones present.

Queen includer fitted

By pinning on the left of the horizontal slot, the queen includer may be slid away from the entrance to allow a queen within to depart; pinning to the right of the slot prevents even accidental sliding of the includer. I've never worked out why there is a vertical slot!

8.5 Drawing Apidea combs in full-size colonies

One appealing idea is to not leave the drawing of combs in an mini-nuc to that cupful of bees, but to have them drawn in a full-size colony. This could provide frames of drawn comb or even sealed brood to assist at establishment, or frames of honey to assure a buffer of stores in each mini-nuc on an ongoing basis. Whilst the latter (stores) works and can be useful in some cases, the former (drawn comb or brood) are more problematic.

With simple modifications to provide internal support, either a National or Modified Commercial shallow frame can accommodate three Apidea frames. This allows the Apidea frames to be placed into a full-size colony for drawing and filling with either brood or stores. We refer to these as **adaptor frames**.

With a couple of slots cut in the side bars, a National shallow frame (14" x 5½") will just allow for three Apidea frames to be squeezed in provided the middle frame rests on the outer two (or vice versa). A Commercial shallow frame (16" x5") is more accommodating, allowing for vertical supports for each Apidea frame, and a Commercial deep (16" x 10") accommodates six well-supported Apidea frames.

Apidea frames measure a whisker over 4½" wide by 4¼" high. Standard British frame sizes are specified by their outer woodwork dimensions and not by the inner comb area. Thus for a quoted 14" x 5½" shallow National frame, the thicknesses of the top bar, two side bars, and the bottom bars all eat into that quoted area. Hence three 4½" wide Apidea frames do not fit within a 14" wide National

Adaptor frame

This National shallow frame has been adapted to take 3 Apidea frames. It is a tight fit; slots cut into the side bars provide some extra space and the outer frames sit slightly above the middle frame to overlap with it. A thin strip of timber is added at the bottom of the frame to better match the Apidea frame height.

frame without cutting into the side bars and arranging that the Apidea frames overlap each other. It's a tight squeeze but do-able. Post Office elastic bands (the ones that your postman so kindly delivers with the post from time to time) yet again prove their usefulness, this time by preventing Apidea frames from sliding sideways out of adaptor frames until they have been propolised into place.

For best results, use brood spacing (35-38mm) for these shallow adaptor frames to match the frame spacing within Apideas. This way the drawn comb will not be too broad to fit when transferred. Shallow Hoffman side bars can be purchased from most equipment suppliers. You can use a few adaptor frames to draw 3, 6, or 9 Apidea frames at a time, or you can make up a full shallow box of 11 adaptor frames to draw 33 Apidea frames in one go.

Be absolutely sure that the full-size colony or colonies chosen are healthy, since any problems here will be transferred to your Apideas.

8.5.1 Frames of empty drawn comb

Why give a tiny Apidea population the task of drawing all their comb from scratch when you could establish them on frames of comb already drawn in a much stronger colony? An appealing idea, but the value of providing ready-made or even ready-filled drawn comb is debatable.

Filling Apideas with drawn comb at establishment hampers the introduction of bees into the inverted Apidea. Instead of being able to tip a cupful of bees in smartly between the open frames of undrawn starter strips, the bees land in a heap on the bottom of the upturned combs, preventing the floor from being slid shut promptly without crushing bees. At most, consider one drawn comb, placed in frame position 3 (closest to the feeder compartment) since this places the comb where the bees will naturally cluster, yet still allows a good aperture for tipping in those bees in the first place.

Assuming that the queen cell given emerges successfully, even if that queen achieves early matings and a swift progression to laying there will be no brood to attend to for

Drawn comb hampers filling with bees

Filling with three frames of drawn comb prevents you from easily tipping in a cupful of bees. Consider using one frame of drawn comb in position 3 (closest to the feeder) as this still allows for a good space within which to tip the bees.

178

Using Apideas

at least a fortnight after establishment. With the feeder full of fondant, nowhere to store incoming forage, and no brood to attend to, workers will readily draw the foundation starter strips into comb in plenty of time for the queen to start laying. Indeed many Apideas have a roughly 2" square patch of comb drawn on frame 3 after the three days in confinement. This mimics the behaviour of a cast swarm, and so feels like we are steering these mating colonies down a more natural route by having them draw their own comb during establishment.

8.5.2   Frames of brood

Sealed brood can be added to an Apidea at any point, provided it has sufficient bees to keep it warm, and the population will receive a great boost when that brood emerges. Sealed brood still produces brood pheromones and hence will promote cohesion and delay the onset of laying workers within short-term queenless Apideas.

Sealed brood combs can also be added to an Apideas at establishment. Only one comb should be added per Apidea, adjacent to the feeder compartment (position 3).

The drone brood problem

When an Apidea adaptor frame is introduced into the brood nest of a strong colony in spring time, they very often choose to raise drone comb, resulting in useless Apidea combs.

179

8 Advanced techniques

The drone brood solution

Insert a brood frame with a 1" starter strip of foundation into the centre of the brood nest. This encourages the colony to satisfy any latent ambition for drone comb and brood, so your Apidea frames will then be drawn as worker comb and laid up with worker brood.

The remaining two frames should have starter strips only so that when the Apidea is inverted for filling, the cupful of bees can still be easily tipped in. Not only does the brood greatly help the new colony to achieve cohesion, the brood comb draws the workers out from the feeder compartment where they cluster closer to the introduced queen cell. Furthermore, if the queen cell given at establishment does not emerge, or the young queen is lost on mating flights, the presence of brood will retain the full population of that mini-nuc until a second ripe queen cell can be given.

Place the shallow adaptor frames amongst standard brood frames, in the centre of the brood nest of a strong colony. The comb will be drawn and quickly laid up. Wait until the brood has been sealed before transferring to Apideas.

To avoid full-size colonies from filling the Apidea frames with drone brood, give those colonies standard brood frames fitted with roughly 1" foundation starter strips. The starter strips can be cut from any old broken foundation sheets, in the same way that we create starter strips for Apidea frames. Place a starter strip frame into the centre of the brood nest and allow it to be drawn and laid up as drone comb before inserting the adaptor frame.

Using Apideas

Bear in mind that the presence of increased drone brood will act as a varroa incubator. It underlines the point that by transferring sealed brood from established colonies into mini-nucs, you may also be introducing varroa mites. One of the subtle benefits of establishing mini-nucs without brood (i.e. just the cupful of bees and foundation to be drawn) is that the only mites introduced are those on the bees themselves.

8.5.3 Frames of stores

In many ways, this is both the easiest and most useful application of having Apidea combs drawn in full-size colonies.

Add the adaptor frames within the centre of the first super on a strong colony (above a queen exlcuder) and they will be rapidly drawn and filled with stores provided there is a flow on (or feed is given). The resulting frames of stores can then be distributed when needed to hungry Apideas. This can be particularly useful if you are running Apideas on 5 frames and hence no longer have the option of feeding fondant. Since these stores frames take time to draw and fill even in a strong host colony, you may find it useful to keep a stock of stores frames prepared in advance if you are going to want to use them regularly.

Do also remember that strong Apideas expanded with an upper brood box may be an easier source of surplus stores on the correct size of frames, and are more likely to be on hand in the mating apiary when you need them.

Frame of honey stores

A surplus frame completely filled with honey can be given to another Apidea as an immediate buffer of stores.

8.6 Over-wintering Apideas

Having stressed that Apideas are for seasonal mating use only, it is indeed possible to overwinter queenright Apideas successfully - even 3-frame Apideas - provided their stores are very closely monitored. These Apideas can give a supply of mated queens for contingency in the spring, particularly if colonies are found to be queenless or contain drone-laying queens at first spring inspection. An Apidea can be united over a queenless colony as described in Chapter 6, *Closing down*.

The greatest risk is that of starvation. Shelter from the wind is a must to prevent undue chilling. Lift the entrance slider right to the top (and use a pin to secure it in this position) to close off the red grille completely, leaving only the entrance hole providing ventilation.

The fondant cartridges in the standard feed compartment are not reliable during cold spells, since workers will not venture that far away from the warmth of the cluster. Instead, run the Apidea without its clear crownboard, and pack fondant into the cavities on the underside of the roof. This provides an accessible source of feed directly above the warmth of the cluster. We call these **roof feeders**.

Check every two weeks and be prepared to replace the roof feeder with another one freshly packed with fondant. Do this as a slick rolling motion, such that the old roof is rolled off to the side in one hand whilst the new roof is rolled into place. For inspiration, watch Indiana Jones heft and exchange a bag of sand for a golden idol at the start of *Raiders of the Lost Ark*. In fact, carry on and watch the whole film again if it's been a while.

Roof packed with fondant

Pack the roof cavities with fondant and remove the crownboard over winter, allowing the bees to feed from directly above the cluster.

Using Apideas

Empty and full roof feeders

The roof cavities can accommodate around 180g of fondant - just two thirds of what is available in a cut comb container feed cartridge. It is essential to check and replace roof feeders regularly.

If the removed roof contains remnants of still-moist fondant, new fondant can be packed around this. The filled roof feeder should then be stored in a zip lock bag (or similar airtight container) to keep the fondant moist pending the next exchange.

The roof cavities can accommodate around 180g of fondant if filled completely as shown here. Compare this with a cut comb feed cartridge holding 280-300g of feed, and you will see why it is important to check and replace roof feeders regularly.

Apideas that have been overwintered become particularly propolised, and their combs significantly darkened by use. Here the lack of strict adherence to beespace in some areas (between frame side bars and inner wall, or the lug end castellations) invites significant propolising that makes them less easy to manipulate. After closing down by uniting, it is worth freezing an empty over-wintered Apidea in order to chip away at any heavy accumulations of propolis before cleaning.

8.7 Temperature monitoring

It can be informative to monitor the temperature of the mini-nucs, either whilst stored in the dark, or whilst out in the mating apiary during a hot summer spell.

Most pet shops sell digital aquarium thermometers for around £10. These are small, battery powered, with a large numeric display and a remote probe on about a metre of thin cable. The remote probe can be inserted under the roof of a mini-nuc for direct monitoring purposes. To avoid problems with propolis or bracing, the probe is placed in the space between the crownboard and the roof; the thin cable easily bends and adapts to allow the roof to be replaced securely.

Minimum and maximum temperatures are logged, meaning you don't need to check every hour through the day and night to ascertain the comfort of the colony. A typical aquarium thermometer displays two temperatures - IN is measured within the thermometer unit itself and is generally the ambient temperature, whilst OUT is measured at the remote probe and is thus the temperature of the monitored mini-nuc. These cheap thermometers are not completely accurate; two identical units placed side by side may disagree by up to a degree. They are good enough for our purposes, though.

We would expect a broodright colony to maintain its brood nest temperature at around 34 - 35°C. By placing the remote probe as described, we are actually measuring the temperature in the un-ventilated but well insulated air gap above the colony. Expect to see readings of 35-36°C here for a normal broodright colony, i.e. a degree or two above the 'textbook' figure.

Using Apideas

Monitoring whilst stored indoors

The thermometer is showing an ambient temperature (IN) a 23.7°C and a temperature at the probe (OUT, i.e. the monitored Apidea) as 28.9°C whilst these Apideas are stored in the dark during establishment.

Monitoring temperatures whilst in the apiary

The thermometer unit is housed in a dummy Apidea on the left, adjacent to the monitored one on the right. The remote probe is placed between the crown board and roof.

In direct sunlight during the hot summer of 2022, this colony recorded a maximum of 38.5°C in the air gap between crownboard and roof.

The black thermometer rapidly warmed up in the sunshine whilst taking pictures so its max IN (ambient) reading of 41.5°C was not accurate!

Monitoring mini-nucs whilst they are stored in the dark is easy - pop the probe under the roof of the chosen colony and stand the thermometer unit on top; check whenever you water the mini-nucs. Monitoring in the apiary requires some means of housing the thermometer unit close to the Apidea since these cheap units are not weatherproof. A simple solution is to use a dummy mini-nuc to house the thermometer body alongside the mini-nuc being monitored,

We often read or hear advice to site Apideas in partial or midday shade to avoid overheating. I believe any such overheating in the British climate is due to a lack of ventilation when the entrance slider is left in the fully up position - i.e. with the red grille completely covered. This is entirely possible in new-ish Apideas where the polystyrene parts are still a snug fit and the beekeeper simply snaps open the entrance slider all the way without thinking of the airflow.

During the hot summer of 2022, we monitored Apideas placed in full sunshine. The more populous units bearded during the hottest parts of the day, but monitoring showed temperatures above the crownboard peaking at 37-39°C. Colonies showed no long-term detriment: queens were mated, brood continued to be raised, combs did not sag, and none of the colonies absconded. I think this demonstrates the effectiveness of the ventilation provided by having the entrance slider closed down to just the 'generous beespace' provided by a push-pin, retaining good ventilation through the red grille. It is uncommon for colonies to significantly restrict this grille with propolis, indicating that they do not object to this level of ventilation even during typically cool British summers.

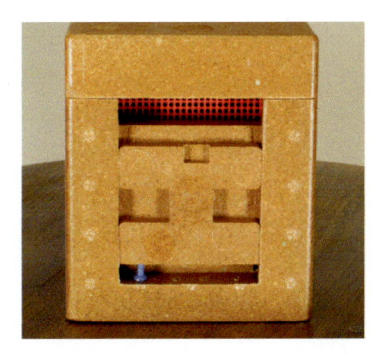

Entrance slider supported by a push pin

A push pins maintains beespace for access at the entrance but still allows for plenty of ventilation through the exposed portion of the red grille.

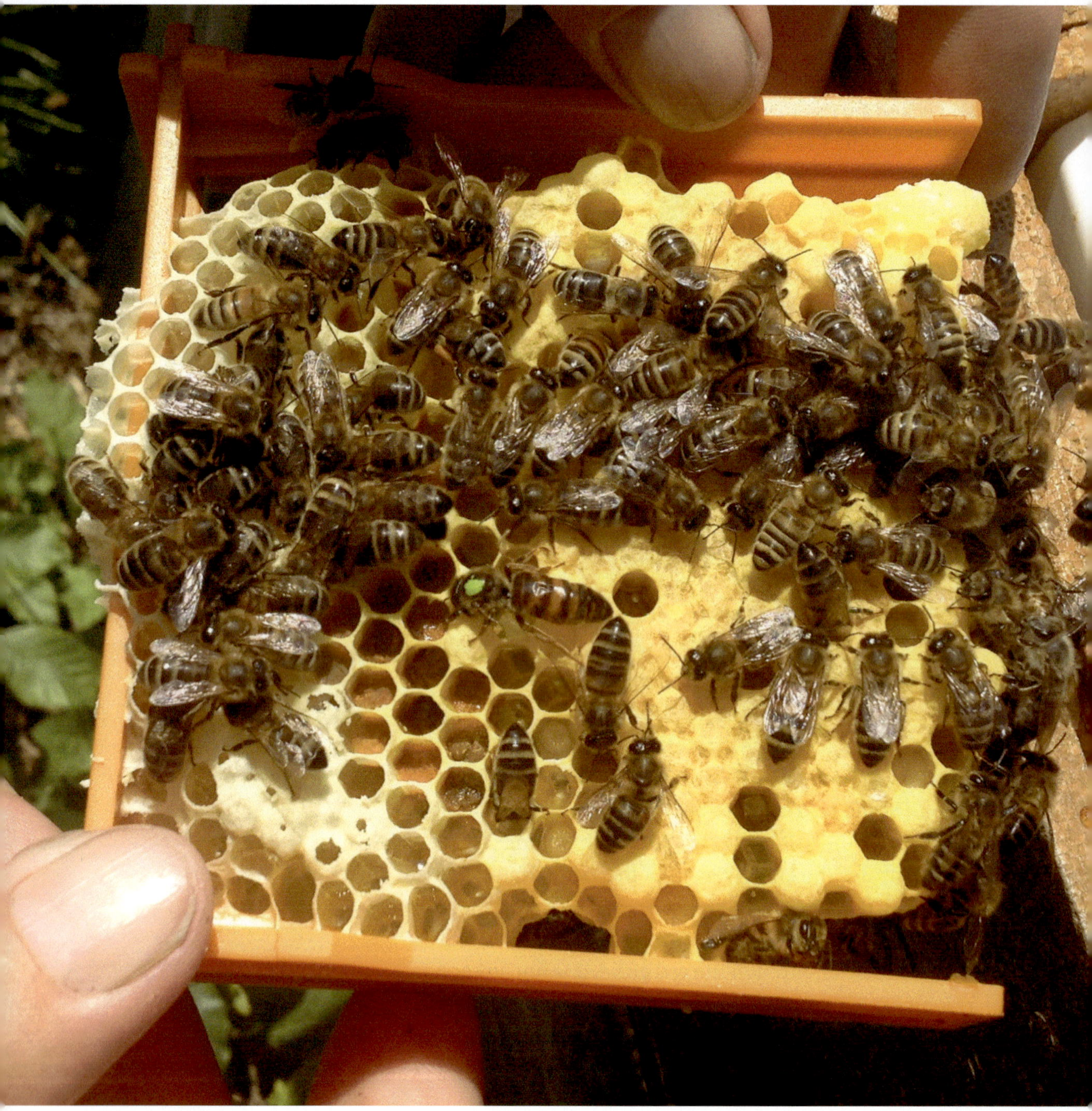

9 Disease and pests

Within the potentially stressful conditions of a small mating nuc colony, any susceptibility to disease should be readily apparent. Ensure that you stock your mini-nucs from healthy colonies, and immediately close down and empty out any mini-nuc that show signs of disease. Be mindful also of pests who may see these small colonies as easy targets for a free meal or a cosy home.

We are using these mini-nucs to house and mate transient queens, so it is more important than normal that the populations of the mini-nucs are healthy. Firstly, there is a risk of exposing the young queen to the disease pathogen, which may be carried by her when she is moved onwards. Secondly, a diseased queen may be inherently inferior even if she does not transfer the disease to her new colony. Thirdly, the burden of any disease is an unnecessary strain on such a small colony as that in an Apidea.

Thankfully, disease problems are rare because beekeepers usually raise queens using only their best colonies. Pests, on the other hand, can strike even the healthiest mini-nucs, often destroying the colony and causing the loss of one of your precious new queens.

9.1 Hygiene

Due to the small number of bees required to stock a mini-nuc, it is entirely possible to stock a couple of dozen mini-nucs in one go from the same, strong, colony. Clearly we want to use healthy bees, so should not stock from colonies with either visual signs or a past history of diseases.

Where a set of mini-nucs have been stocked from the same donor colony, we assume that each of those mini-nucs is as healthy or unhealthy as any other. Hence the risks of interventions such as moving brood between them should be minimal. If multiple donor colonies have been used, then we are reliant on each donor colony being equally healthy. As successive batches of mini-nucs are stocked from different colonies, we take bees from other healthy colonies, but consider for management purposes that the mini-nucs are a cohesive group, equally healthy at the outset. Thus moving frames of brood or stores around, or the various methods of bolstering adult populations, are considered low-risk as long as the mini-nucs remain healthy. Given the frequency with which mini-nucs are inspected, and the attention that we are paying to the contents of very small areas of comb, any problems should be immediately apparent - and should be addressed immediately whilst still localised.

9.2   Dealing with disease

Should any disease occur, the afflicted Apidea is closed up that evening, removed from the mating apiary and placed in a domestic deep freeze for 48 hours to kill the colony. We do not simply shake the bees out, since they would disperse around the other Apideas and hives in the mating apiary, taking the disease pathogen with them.

The combs are melted down, any remaining fondant securely disposed of, and all hive parts are scraped, washed, and then sterilised by submerging in a bleach solution. After this, the Apidea can be put back into use.

I discuss how we clean our Apideas in detail in Chapter 10, *Maintenance*.

Do not be tempted to use petrol to kill a colony in an Apidea, since petrol dissolves the polystyrene.

9.3 Varroa

Look carefully at the queen shown at the start of this chapter, and it becomes apparent that she has deformed wings and a deformed abdomen - the result of Varroa mite damage during her development.

Clearly such a queen cannot fly to mate, yet the bees surrounding her do not realise this flaw until several weeks have passed, when they will become increasingly aggressive towards her, ultimately disposing of the queen and leaving themselves hopelessly queenless. Any queen who emerges into a mini-nuc with deformed wings should be promptly removed and the mini-nuc treated as if the queen cell failed to emerge - recycle by introducing another ripe queen cell at the earliest opportunity.

Varroa damage to a queen emerging into a mini-nuc results from mites in the queen raising colony, not in the mini-nuc. On occasion you might see a queen in a mating nuc with deformed wings. With careful monitoring and control (when appropriate) of mites in the queen raisers, we see only one or two deformed queens each season.

Ensure also that mite levels are low within the donor colony or colonies prior to establishing mini-nucs. Do not burden the mini-nucs with an unnecessary mite load that will impair the tiny colony and propagate viral diseases. This may mean an 'out of sequence' application of Varroa controls for the donor colonies compared to other colonies where mite levels are generally higher after a mild winter. Any drone raising colonies must be actively monitored and managed for Varroa, since they are potential mite incubators, impacting the supply and quality of drones mating with your newly-raised queens.

Using Apideas

9.4 Chalkbrood

The fungal spores responsible for Chalkbrood disease are widespread amongst honey bee colonies. The conditions required for chalkbrood to flare up are a reduced brood nest temperature and increased CO_2 levels - essentially what happens when a small colony is under stress and struggling to maintain optimal brood nest conditions.

We see a case of chalkbrood every two or three years in our Apideas. In that respect it is rare, but still the most common disease that we have observed. An affected Apidea would be closed down immediately as described earlier in this chapter. Importantly, we do not cause or allow the bees to disperse to other mini-nucs nearby, to minimise the risk of disease spread.

To reduce potential chalkbrood problems, we never source bees for establishment from colonies with any history of chalkbrood.

Chalkbrood mummies

The grey/white pellets on the floor of this Apidea confirm chalkbrood disease.

9.5 Nosema

Nosema disease, like chalkbrood, is caused by a widespread pathogen, and disease occurrence is associated with stressed colonies. With *Nosema ceranae*, there can be high levels of infection with no apparent signs of distress – certainly none of the fouling or dysentery often associated with *Nosema apis*.

A queen living amongst Nosema-infected workers could easily become infected herself; it will impair her digestion of protein, and may restrict her laying ability. If a queen and workers from a Nosema-infected mini-nuc are caged together for introduction, there is also a possibility that they could transmit the disease to the colony to which they are introduced.

We prefer to check a sample of adult bees under the microscope before declaring even a strong colony to be a suitable donor for establishing mini-nucs. With this approach, we cannot recall an incident of nosema disease in our Apideas.

9.6 Wasps

For us, August marks the imminent end of mini-nuc usage because the wasps are suddenly out robbing in force. Left unhindered, wasps can overrun and strip out a mini-nuc a day, rapidly laying waste to your mating apiary.

Whilst wasps are beneficial for ten months of the year, in July and August they are a considerable threat to small honey bee colonies. These wasps are hungry for an alternative food source as their nests naturally decline, seeking out any readily accessible sweet food. This is when they suddenly become interested in cream teas, glasses of cider, and weak honeybee colonies. Trapping of wasps in late summer can buy you time to complete your queen matings.

Various manufactured wasp traps are available and by all accounts work, but being beekeepers we tend to adapt and re-use. Having started with 2lb jam/pickle jars and pencil-sized holes punched in the metal lids, experimentation showed that the yellow 'Vaso Trap' hornet trap lids were significantly more effective - and conveniently fit those same 2lb jars.

Soiling around the entrance

Dysentery such as this may be caused by Nosema or by the consumption of fermenting stores. Checking some adult bees under the microscope will give a reliable diagnosis.

Using Apideas

Wasp trap lids compared

Three jars with the same bait dotted about on hive roofs in the same apiary during August. The effectiveness of the *Vaso Trap* lid compared with punched jar lids was clear.

Release trapped hornets

We employ the latest digital technique to release any European hornets inadvertently caught in the wasp traps.

These jars are easy to manage and can be startlingly effective at trapping wasps, but with the lids being designed as hornet traps, the mouth of the funnel needs to be restricted in order to exclude European hornets – these being of no appreciable threat to the mini-nucs.

Ambrosia is an inverted syrup feed formulated for honey bees, and has the interesting property of having a scent of almost no interest to honey bees, whilst simultaneously being catnip for wasps. This makes for a highly selective bait for wasp traps. I find the other major inverted syrup sold as bee feed, Belgosuc, is less selective in attractiveness.

The commercially sold wasp baits can be surprisingly poor in comparison to either inverted syrup or plan old home-mixed granulated white sugar syrup. I was particularly disappointed by the purple Suterra / Trappit as a wasp bait (its stated purpose!), having previously purchased some of this at great expense to use in monitoring for Asian Hornets.

9 Disease and pests

Whilst sugar syrup is appealing - cheap, easy to mix as & when needed - it has one major disadvantage: it also attracts honey bees, particularly when the main summer flow has ended. Fortunately, as sugar syrup begins to ferment, its attractiveness to honey bees reduces greatly whilst at the same time becoming more attractive to wasps. Thus we make up a ten litre container of syrup in June and leave it out in the sun in the honey farm yard to allow it to ferment. By leaving the cap very slightly unscrewed, any gassing can vent away without causing the container to bulge. By July, this syrup is ready for use as soon as the wasps start worrying the Apideas.

Once fermented syrup traps have been in use for a fortnight and dead wasps within them have started to decay, the resulting 'juice' can be added to fresh syrup to rapidly start fermentation and increase attractiveness to wasps whilst reducing the syrup's appeal to honey bees.

In our comparative tests, Ambrosia and sugar syrup performed equally well, but it was this 'fresh syrup and

Baits compared

After three days of testing during heavy wasp robbing of unoccupied nuc boxes in the honey farm yard, the relative attractiveness of each bait was apparent:

1. Suterra / Trappit, costly commercial wasp bait
2. Fermenting sugar syrup (1:1 mix)
3. Sugar syrup & 'juice' from an established trap
4. Ambrosia

juice' mixture that proved the most attractive to wasps. However making this mixture does necessitate waiting a couple of weeks for the first batch of syrup to ferment, and then another couple of weeks for a good 'juice' to be available. Ambrosia is not quite as attractive but offers the major advantage of immediate efficacy, yet it does not ferment or denature when stored in a cool dry shed, so can simply be dispensed as and when needed.

Place a number of wasp trap jars around and between the mating nucs. Each time you visit the mating apiary, take a kitchen sieve and a bucket with you. Empty each full wasp trap jar through the sieve, catching the liquid bait in the bucket; jars can then be refilled from the bucket. Turn the wasp corpses out onto clear ground away from the hives, and spread the pile with the sieve so that you can check for Asian hornets if you are using un-restricted vaso trap lids.

If you are seeing noticeable numbers of honey bees trapped, do not re-establish the wasp trap jars until you have changed your bait for one less attractive to bees. Apideas do not need to lose many bees to be significantly weakened.

If wasps are particularly prevalent, use a decoy mini-nuc for wasp trapping A honey jar will fit into an Apidea and so can be used as a wasp trap with a pencil-sized hole punched through its lid. Part-fill this jar with bait and place inside an Apidea that has been emptied of frames. Leave this decoy mini-nuc on the edge of the apiary, a little way away from the others so that it appears more vulnerable. Be prepared to empty this wasp trap jar regularly.

9 Disease and pests

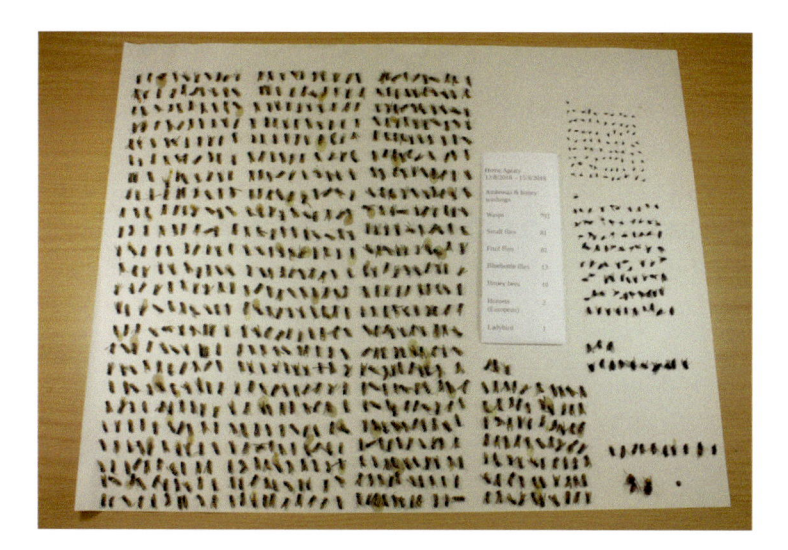

Concern has been expressed recently over insect by-catch when trapping, in the context of Asian Hornet monitoring. We examined a large number of wasp trap jars during the 2018 season, to understand the impact our trapping was having. The one shown here is typical: it appears to be a jar full of yellow/black wasp bodies. When emptied and sorted the majority were indeed wasps - almost 800 of them. The many fruit flies captured were attracted to the fallen fruit in an orchard of several hundred apple trees, next to the apiary.

We do not consider the number of flies trapped to be detrimental to the local ecology - repeated trapping in subsequent years does not appear to have had any impact on late summer fly numbers at this site. If syrup trapping on this scale were effective as a fly control, then the pig, poultry and equestrian industries would have adopted it wholesale years ago. We do, however, believe that the trapping of significant numbers of wasps has been of great benefit to the honey bee colonies sited here.

Catch assessed

This typical trap was tipped out and its contents rinsed, dried, sorted and counted:

    793 wasps
    175 assorted flies
    10 honey bees
    2 European hornets
    1 ladybird

The photo shows how these were grouped for counting on a sheet of flip chart paper, and amply demonstrates how many wasps had been caught.

196

9.7 Badgers

Where mini-nucs are placed at (or close to) ground level, they can be prone to badger damage if discovered. Badgers are skillful and polite opportunists. They learn to roll the hives over to scatter their contents, and will chew out the combs without damaging the frames, but it's still fatal to the colony.

The nutritious combs - wax, honey, pollen, and brood - are an appealing meal for a badger and it will return on subsequent nights to turn over and consume more mini-nucs.

Simply lifting the mini-nucs to a comfortable working height on tables or posts avoids this 'badger buffet' problem. They reputedly have poor eyesight and appear to have no inclination to climb or to investigate the scent of hives when placed out of reach.

9 Disease and pests

Badger damage

Mini-nucs located close to the ground may be rolled over and clawed open by badgers, who savour the nutritious combs and will return for more the following evening. Those above were standing on upturned shallow plastic crates; Apidea parts and frames lie strewn across the ground, with combs completely chewed out.

9.8 Mice

Mice are generally not an issue with mini-nucs being managed in the active season – spring and summer – but may attack the entrances of over-wintering mini-nucs, chewing at the polystyrene to gain access. Once in, they will chew away combs, plastic, and polystyrene in order to construct a nest. Clearly this is fatal for the colony within the mini-nuc, scuppering your plan to over-winter that colony and queen. Keeping over-wintering mini-nucs high up - such as on pallet table - can be a deterrent.

Of perhaps more concern than in-season damage is the effect that mice or rats can have on stored polystyrene equipment in general: they can and will chew through and shred it if there is anything tasty left within. Traces of old comb or even fondant are appealing to rodents. Thus it is advisable to store mini-nucs clean, empty of comb or feed residues, ideally in a rodent-proof building or container. The same can be said, of course, of any polystyrene beehive equipment.

9 Disease and pests

Mouse damage

Mice will readily chew through the polystyrene around the entrance to gain access in the autumn. Construction of their nest destroys the colony, and their gnawing at both polystyrene and plastic parts can render a mini-nuc unusable.

9.9 Wax moth

Rarely seen in active mini-nucs, greater wax moth can be devastating for stored mini-nucs. They will chew tunnels through the polystyrene in any direction, perforating mini-nucs like colanders.

I learnt this lesson the hard way. If you buy Apideas in bulk, they come packed 18 to a large cardboard box, which makes for easy storage in the winter. However one year I managed to pack away one Apidea with residual brood comb by mistake in amongst 17 properly cleaned ones. By the time I realised what had happened next spring it was too late – the wax moth larvae had simply burrowed from Apidea to Apidea in all directions, perforating as they went.

By stripping out a set of undamaged parts and using wood filler repairs, I think I salvaged about 8 usable Apideas from the 18. I keep the 'source' Apidea carcass in my "rogue's gallery" to show students on our queen raising courses and hopefully prevent them from making the same mistake!

The simple precaution of removing used brood comb and cleaning mini-nucs before storage will remove the attractiveness and hence reduce the chance of wax moth destruction to virtually nil.

9 Disease and pests

Wax moth damage

If old brood combs are left within Apideas stored over winter, greater wax moth larvae will dig into and tunnel through the polystyrene. In an extreme case such as this, Apideas can be rendered virtually unusable. Remove used comb before storage!

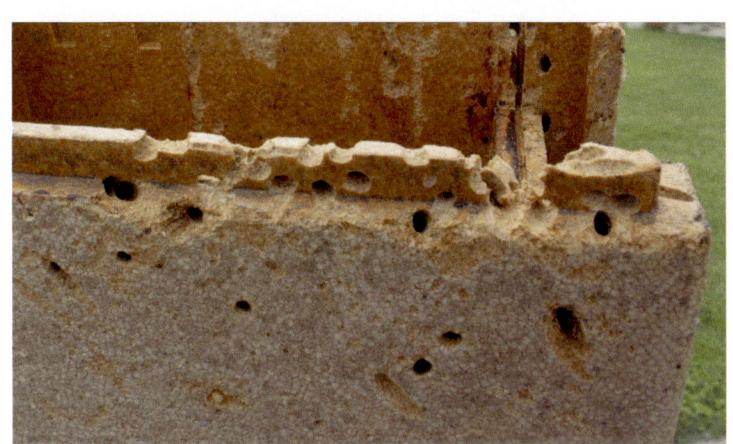

9.10 Woodpeckers

In some areas, green woodpeckers can be a considerable winter problem for beekeepers. They target hives, pecking large holes in the side so that they can reach within to consume bees, brood, and stores. Only over-wintered mini-nucs should be susceptible to woodpecker problems, but the colony is likely to be rapidly overwhelmed by chilling or damp if the mini-nuc is holed.

Prevention of woodpecker attack is the same for mini-nucs as for any other hive - use polythene sheets or chicken-wire cages. The portability of mini-nucs means they could also readily be moved to a different apiary that does not suffer from woodpecker attacks.

Because of the concentrated nature of woodpecker pecking, it can be possible to repair even quite extensively damaged mini-nucs. Indeed the Apidea shown to the right was repaired with successive applications of wood filler built up to close the larger holes, then painted over to protect the filler patches from the elements.

9 Disease and pests

Woodpecker damage

Over-wintering mini-nucs may be susceptible to damage by green woodpeckers. The polystyrene easily yields to pecking and the colony is destroyed by a combination of predation and exposure.

204

205

10 Maintenance

Apideas need to be cleaned thoroughly between seasons, and do get damaged, whether through wear and tear, mishap, or pest problems. It is possible to repair light damage to both polystyrene and plastic parts. Due to the modular nature of Apideas, even severely damaged hives can usually be stripped of some useful spares. Repairs can be fiddly and time-consuming; as ever, weigh up the time incurred against the cost of replacement.

Mini-nucs should be cleaned before re-use or storage, for hygienic reasons. At the end of season, clean all your Apideas thoroughly, both to ensure that they are ready for use next season, but also to ensure they will be easy to handle, without obstructive deposits of wax or propolis. Stripping Apideas to their component parts also highlights any minor repairable damage.

Once clean, it is important that you store Apideas with precautions against the two main pests of unoccupied hive equipment: wax moths and rodents. An infestation of either can rapidly reduce stored Apideas to unusable scrap.

When your queen raising starts again next season, you will be reaching for Apideas during the busiest part of the season. It greatly streamlines the queen raising workload if your Apideas are stacked clean and ready for use - just take the ones you need and stock them.

Polystyrene suffers ultraviolet damage through exposure to sunlight. This causes the bubbles of the polystyrene outer surfaces to collapse slightly, leading to a roughened, bleached, and crumbly surface. A simple remedy is to paint the outer surfaces with a masonry paint. Ideally paint Apideas from new, but painting will effectively halt further degradation in hives that have already been weathered.

10.1 Cleaning Apideas

Dismantle each Apidea into its component parts, and clean the various plastic and polystyrene parts as follows:

Scrape - scraping with a hive tool (or similar) removes lightly attached wax and propolis debris. Take care not to dig into the polystyrene or plastic.

Freeze - if debris is stubborn (particularly propolis) then freeze parts overnight and repeat the scraping. The cold, brittle wax and propolis should come away easily now.

Soak - some debris is inaccessible, such as propolis or wax deposited within the grilles and apertures of the red plastic parts. Soak these parts in a washing soda solution for 48 hours. Use an old 30lb lidded plastic honey bucket, half-filled with a strong washing soda solution. Throw all the parts in to soak, ensure the lid is on tight, then shake the whole bucket to ensure the parts are dispersed.

Scrub - scrub the various parts in a warm washing soda solution with a plastic washing up brush to remove any remaining traces of wax or propolis.

Bleach - if you wish to sterilise plastic or polystyrene parts, submerge them in a 1:5 bleach:water solution and soak for 20 minutes. Small draw-string net bags allow many plastic parts to be submerged together.

Rinse - thoroughly rinse all parts to remove any traces of washing soda or bleach.

This may sound like quite a performance, but really it's a straightforward and methodical approach to cleaning. At the end of the beekeeping season, I set myself up a

Washing soda bucket
Various plastic Apidea and queen raising parts are soaking in a washing soda solution for 48 hours to soften wax and propolis deposits.

10 Maintenance

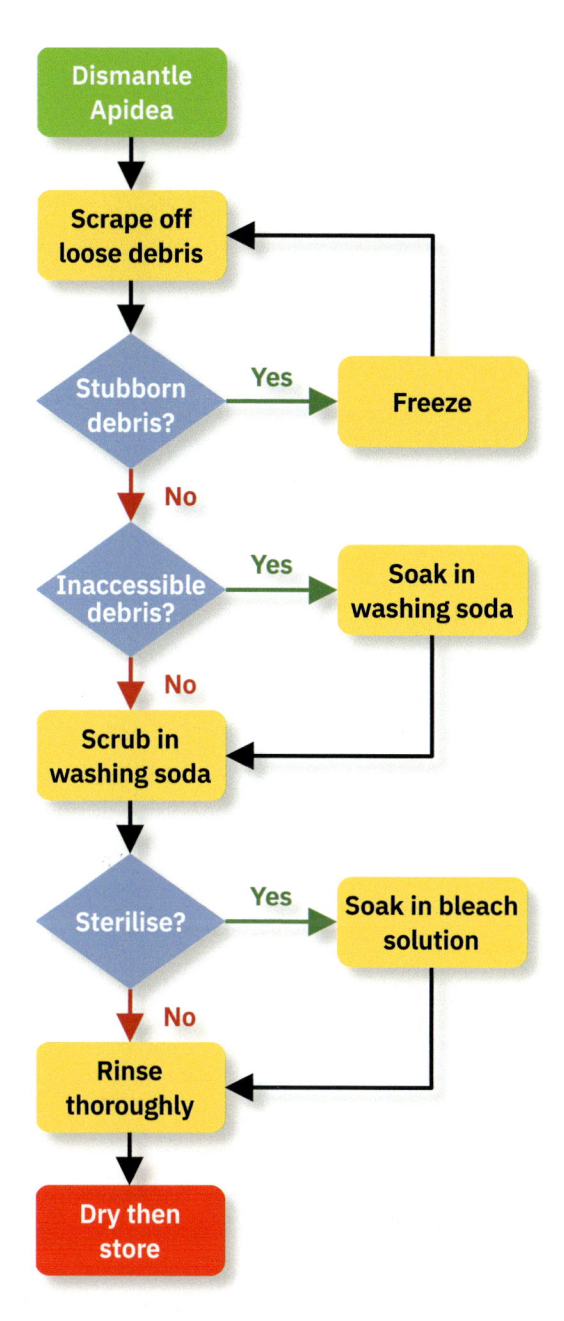

The cleaning process

The flowchart applies to cleaning every part of a dismantled Apidea.

temporary workbench for this job in one of the sheds. A couple of pallets nearby allow me to stack the washed and

Using Apideas

Temporary cleaning bench

A simple bench set up with a large plastic crate of warm washing soda. Apideas are stacked ready for dismantling and cleaning. The white buckets are for (left) a washing soda soak and (right) comb removed from frames. The cardboard box was for feed containers, which were cleaned later. Parts were stacked for drying on an adjacent pallet as shown at the start of this chapter.

rinsed components to dry - as shown at the start of this chapter. It's a nice warm job for a cool day!

Dismantling is straightforward. You will need various containers for removed wax comb, pins, dried fondant, and so on, plus a washing soda soak bucket to hand. In terms of scraping tools, a 3" wallpaper scraper and either a slender J-tool or a 1" straight decorator's tool are ideal.

The red plastic parts are the easiest to clean. These can be scraped, soaked in a washing soda solution, lightly scrubbed to remove wax, propolis, and other debris, and then rinsed thoroughly.

Frames may also be cleaned in a similar fashion. First remove any comb: flex side bars outwards to detach the comb then twist the comb to break it away from the top bar. Dismantle frames into their three component parts, and use a hive tool or scraper to lightly remove excess remaining wax. Place side bars straight into the wash bucket to soften the remaining wax.

10 Maintenance

Attaching foundation starter strips with molten wax can leave quite a substantial deposit of wax on the underside of the frame top bars. If you find such deposits, put these top bars aside and freeze them overnight, then use a hive tool or similar scraper to carefully remove the now brittle wax deposits whilst still cold – they should easily detach from the plastic.

With minimal remaining wax, the washing soda will bring frame parts up clean again. Soak, scrub, and rinse all frame parts.

Do not be tempted to shortcut the process and boil-wash frames – the orange frames will warp and become useless. If you wish to be able to boil wash frames, invest in the blue frames available from equipment dealers, which will survive being boiled.

One season I hit upon the idea of placing red plastic parts, frame parts, queen cages and Cupkit parts into small draw-string net bags (as sold for washing delicate fabric items) and placing these in the washing machine with a cup of washing soda, extra rinse and no spin. It worked well for several batches of parts one season, but was it merely coincidence that the washing machine's drum bearings failed before that season was out? Of course, the bearings were essentially irreplaceable and hence a mere ten year old washing machine had to be scrapped. I've not repeated the experiment!

The National Bee Unit's fact sheet *Hive Cleaning and Sterilisation* (available from their website, www.nationalbeeunit.com) details various cleaning and sterilisation methods for wooden and polystyrene beehives.

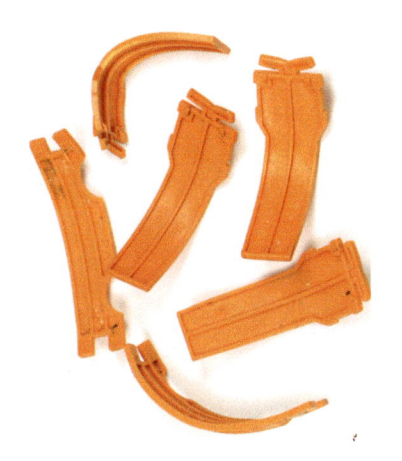

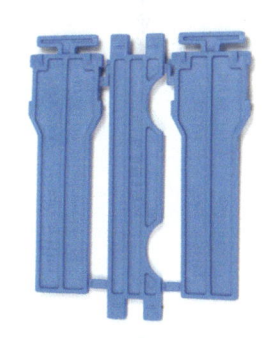

Standard Apidea frames are warped by boiling

The standard orange Apidea frames do not withstand boiling water. Blue frames are available that can be safely boil washed, if necessary.

210

I only sterilise Apideas where there have been disease problems, or where a colony has died out, but in these instances all parts will be first cleaned as detailed above and then submerged in a bleach solution for 20 minutes. The National Bee Unit advises that this should be a mix of 1 part domestic bleach to 5 parts of water. For this part of the process, eye protection, gloves, and good ventilation are essential.

Once cleaned, I reassemble all the bodies with floors, entrance sliders, crown boards, and roofs. The frames stay dismantled in a box until needed for assembly, and the red plastic parts are sorted into different pots and trays. This makes for easy storage over winter and quick assembly in spring ready for establishment.

Sterilising in bleach solution
This previously scraped and scrubbed Apidea hive body is being soaked in a bleach solution in order to sterilise it. The brick keeps it submerged.

10.2 Repairs

Over time various parts of your Apideas will become worn or broken. In some cases effective repairs can be made, in others repairs are not durable and replacement is more effective.

If you are completely dismantling your Apideas for the annual winter clean-up, as we do, any irreparable breakages are disposed of. After re-assembly, surplus usable parts are stored for later re-use. Whilst individual spare parts are indeed available to purchase, you may find it simpler and cheaper to buy a couple of new Apideas from time to time as either complete replacements or to dismantle as a stock of parts.

As we rarely have problems with woodpeckers, and learnt the lesson of wax moth damage long ago, over time we have accumulated a small surplus of Apidea hive bodies and roofs, these being the parts generally least susceptible to wear and tear.

10.2.1 Frame repairs

The usual damage that occurs to the plastic frames is that a side bar lug eventually snaps off during periodic disassembly and reassembly of frames. We lose a couple of side bars a season to this type of breakage during the winter clean-up.

Due to the snap-fit nature of the sidebar -to-topbar joint, gluing the snapped pieces is not effective. Maintain a stock of spare frames and accept that there will be some breakages over time through repeated handling.

Broken frame parts

The lugs of the sidebars may snap after repeated handling. Unfortunately as a snap-fit part they cannot be glued; keep a stock of replacement frames.

10.2.2 Polystyrene repairs

Damaged polystyrene can be repaired with wood filler. Careful repair work will be needed if the damage is on mating or moving surfaces where two parts meet or slide, and such damage may quickly render the part beyond practical repair. Look for a wood filler that can be sanded when it has cured, this will allow you to fine-tune any repairs. Most wood fillers are water-based and need to be sealed with paint, otherwise they will weather rapidly and disintegrate.

Polystyrene repair

Woodpecker damage to this roof was repaired by building up wood filler to close the hole. This was a straightforward repair as it involved no moving or mating surfaces.

After sanding, the repair was sealed by repainting the roof with masonry paint. This repair has lasted for at least six seasons now.

Eventually you will encounter damage caused by wax moth, who will chew through the polystyrene and embed their cocoons in the resulting crevices and tunnels. Wood filler is ideal for patching up even quite dramatically holed parts, as long as the damage has not greatly eroded those mating or moving surfaces. A grafting tool makes short work of dragging out any embedded wax moth cocoons prior to repair. However if your mini-nuc resembles a colander it may better to scrap it – but keep any remaining serviceable parts such as frames and grilles as spares.

10.2.3 Clear plastic repairs

Most commonly, the labels used to attach the flaps over the crownboard holes weaken and tear with repeated use. 1" lengths cut from a roll of 2" gaffer or duct tape make for durable replacements.

I have one crownboard which split along its length - quite how evades me - and that has survived for several seasons now taped up with clear 2" parcel tape. The tape is durable whilst in use, but comes unstuck after soaking in washing soda so is replaced at each annual cleaning.

The crownboards do yellow noticeably and buckle slightly over a number of years. This can't be UV damage, and may be either gentle degradation over time or an adverse reaction to the washing soda, particularly when soaked. It is not a varnish of propolis - the washing soda would dissolve this. The yellowing does not greatly impair visibility through the crownboards, rather the buckling (if pronounced) can lead to them slipping about in use. Again, I buy some spares about every ten years and replace any unserviceable ones.

Crownboard flap repairs

Here the clear flaps have been reattached using strips of duct tape when the label 'hinges' tore. You can also see the progressive yellowing - the crownboards start life clear and colourless.

10.2.4 Red plastic repairs

Over the years I have naturally broken a number of the red plastic pieces. The small includers and excluders are not easy to repair, since they have very few contact points to glue them firmly and accurately.

The large red grilles can be glued successfully. There are many contact point along the break, so glue provides a durable repair. Both polystyrene cement or superglue work equally well.

10 Maintenance

10.3 Painting

Polystyrene degrades over time due to sunlight exposure. The surface bleaches and the outermost bubbles start to collapse, becoming brittle and prone to wear. I have found smooth masonry paint to be excellent for painting over polystyrene hives, and it is durable, surviving 6-8 seasons before re-painting is needed. A litre of paint will cover up to 24 Apideas in two coats each. Only paint the outside!

Clean and dry your Apideas before painting. Assemble floors, bodies and roofs for ease of handling; entrance sliders are easier to paint separately. Use a 2" brush to get quick and accurate coverage of the major surfaces, and a smaller artist's brush to do the detail work. IKEA sell a pack of six kids' paint brushes (MÅLA, £3.50) that includes a 15mm flat brush that is ideal for this purpose.

Avoid working paint along and into joint lines, such as between the hive body and roof. Once the first coat of paint has dried, crack open the roof, floor, and entrance slider (if appropriate) before adding the second coat. This stops hive parts getting glued together by paint. Do not paint the sliding edges of the entrance sliders, or the grooves in the hive body in which they slide. Once dry, any heavy paint accumulations at joints can be trimmed back with a sharp blade held flat against the polystyrene.

10.3.1 Paint colours

Where many mating nucs are to be used in close proximity, it may aid navigation if the nucs are different colours. Bees navigate very accurately by shape, orientation, and relative placement of hives, but you can

Dyed masonry paint

30g sample sachets of powdered cement dye are mixed with white masonry paint - notice how much lighter the paint colours are even when saturated with dye. We have found the Sandtex smooth masonry paint to be very reliable over the years.

216

Using Apideas

add colour cues to assist this. Blues, greens, and yellows are good colours to consider; remember that red is an uninteresting colour for bees.

Masonry paint is generally available in a range of uninspiring colours: grey, white, and fifty shades of beige. Fortunately, white masonry paint can be dyed with powdered cement dyes or liquid paint pigments to give more appropriate colours. I purchase cement dye online, and find a 30g sample sachet will easily colour a litre of masonry paint, and costs about £3 posted. One large tin of white masonry paint can thus be decanted and dyed into several different colours quite cost-effectively.

When trying different mixes and dye proportions, I've found that there is a colour saturation point - adding further dye does not further darken the shade. This saturation results in medium-light shades, noticeably lighter than the dry powder but giving great contrast for marker pen numbering. The powdered dye does tend to stiffen up the paint when fully mixed, so I add a little water to adjust the consistency accordingly.

Painting Apideas

Two coats of masonry paint will survive for 6-8 years before getting scruffy, making it a very cost- and time-effective measure.

The three colours shown mixed on the previous page are shown here when they have dried on the Apideas.

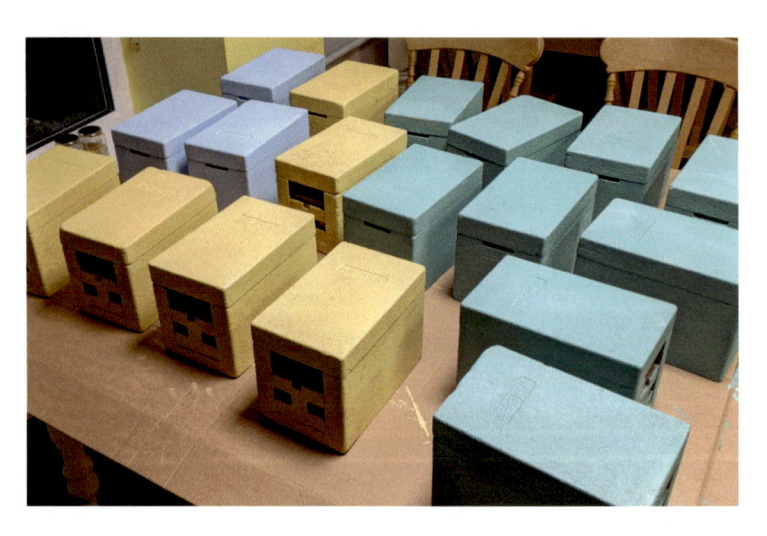

If you wish to have more variability of colours, divide your Apideas into three sets, and paint each set either blue, yellow, or green. Once the paint has dried, strip all three sets to their obvious component parts (body, roof, entrance slider), jumble, and reassemble. This will give many possible colourways for each Apidea – harlequin hives!

The recommended placement of ten Apideas to a pallet described in chapter 2, *Getting Ready* has not resulted in obvious or damaging levels of queens lost on mating flights, but a small number of such losses do happen. Relative hive placement and entrance orientation must be strong navigational cues even when closely-packed Apideas are all the same colour, but can colour differences enhance this? It is often seen deployed in photos of busy mating apiaries. I have been preparing our Apideas as shown for testing next season. They were due for a re-paint, so I took the opportunity to experiment. I will run tables of same colour Apideas, and tables of harlequin Apideas, and see if there is any discernible change in queen losses on mating flights.

Harlequin hives

By jumbling up the pieces of the painted hives, they can be reassembled in many more colour variations. Next year's experiment is to see if this reduces queens lost on mating flights. I've painted about thirty like this, to compare with the uniformly coloured Apideas.

Using Apideas

10.4 Spare parts

A few equipment dealers sell a number of spare parts for Apideas. The red plastic parts are prone to loss or damage, especially the large red ventilation grille or the small queen excluder for the feeder access slot. You can also buy packs of additional frames, either to keep as general spares, or for converting from 3-frame to 5-frame operation.

When shopping for Apidea parts, you will come across boil-proof options for the plastic parts, with the most-frequently stocked being the blue boil-proof frames. With the cleaning processes I undertake, I do not have a need to boil such parts.

Usually, individual hive body parts (such as floors, roofs, and entrance sliders) are not available, although some of the more enterprising dealers do sell them. Presumably they simply dismantle and 'part out' new Apideas.

Some European dealers also sell compatible parts that are interchangeable between Apideas and close copies. A notable dealer would be Heinrich Holtermann in Germany, who stock the complete range of Apidea parts and compatible *Rütli* and *MiniApi* mating nucs and parts. I have checked their compatibility by stripping an Apidea and a Rütli, and interchanging all parts. This opens up further replacement options, including 'boil proof' replacements for the various red plastic parts of the Apidea.

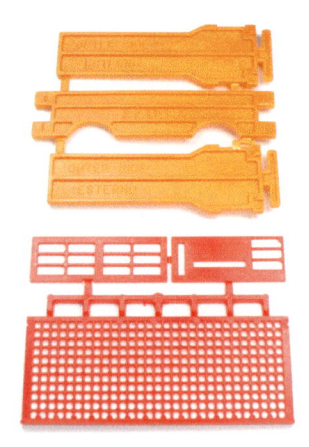

Spare parts

It's wise to keep a number of spares to hand. Frames and red plastic parts are readily available.

10.5 Storage

You should also be very mindful of wax moth and rodent damage when storing Apideas (or any polystyrene hive parts).

The larvae of greater wax moth can destroy stored polystyrene mini-nucs. Think of the hollowing-out that they do in woodwork – the softer polystyrene is easier to chew through and they can quickly perforate and tunnel through the material. Any wax moth infested mini-nucs may well be rendered uneconomic to repair.

To avoid problems with wax moth, you need to be sure that there is no old brood comb left in stored Apideas. It is relatively easy to overlook one stored mini-nuc with such combs still in place, and not only will that mini-nuc be perforated but often the surrounding ones will also be damaged. I mentioned elsewhere about losing many of a box of 18 Apideas packed together due to wax moth larvae tunnelling in all directions from the initially infested hive.

I take care to store the Apideas in a rodent-proof shed. I know of one bee farmer who lost about forty Apideas to rats one winter. They were stored in a lean-to, behind other beekeeping equipment, and were quietly shredded - not a single usable one remained.

Using Apideas

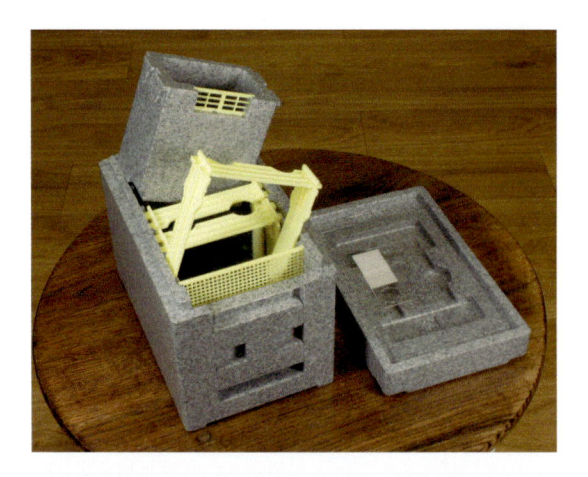

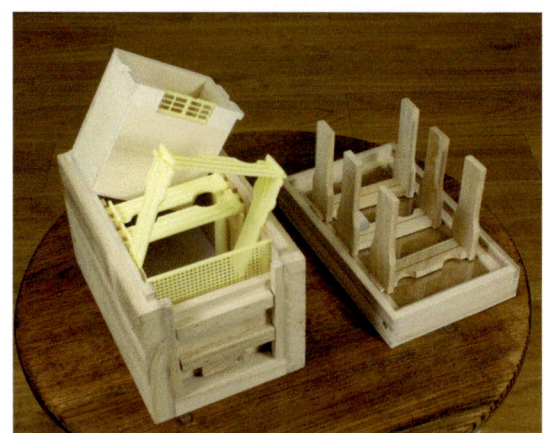

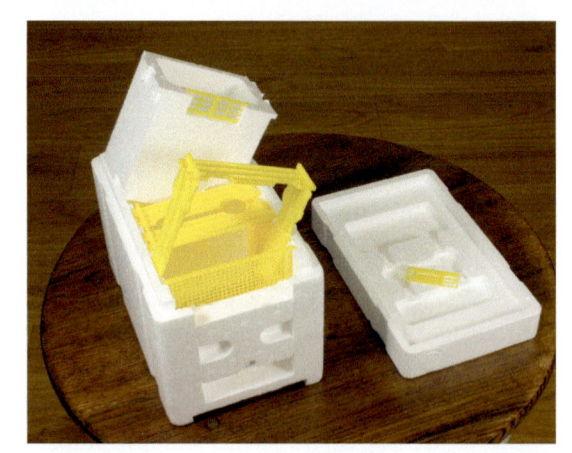

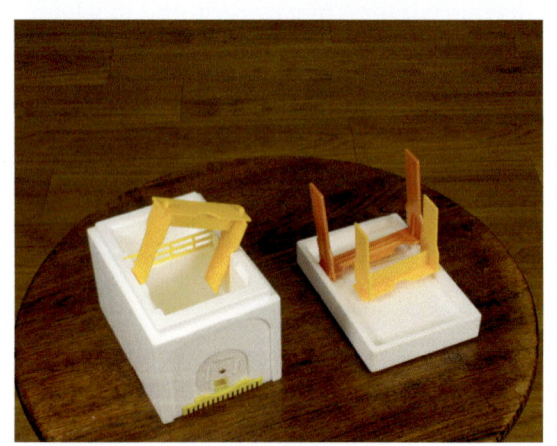

221

11 Clones & imitators

In preparing for this book, I have acquired several similar mini mating nucs for comparison. On the following pages, I will look at the pros and cons of each of these commonly available mini-nucs.

Whilst all Apideas still carry a Swiss patent number moulded into the underside of the roof, that patent was filed in 1982 and consequently expired twenty years later. Thus since 2002 it has been legal to copy the Apidea.

Some copies are clearly produced to a lower price point. It often appears that the each difference in the detail of these imitators is a change for the worse: individually slight, but cumulatively these differences make for a significantly less satisfying experience.

None of these derivatives are as elegant as the Apidea. Indeed the only one that does match up is, essentially, a direct copy. Perhaps this is why the term 'Apidea' is now almost the generic term, used to describe any of these small poly mating nucs, much as with 'Hoover' or 'Jeep'.

Using Apideas

11.1 Earlier and later pattern Apideas

These two Apideas were produced some forty years apart. There are some detail changes, but the fundamental pattern has remained the same, to the extent that the earlier and later parts are fully interchangeable, indicating how well suited the Apidea was as a mini mating nuc from the outset.

As noted in the introduction, our surviving earlier pattern Apideas had become completely dispersed in amongst the later patterns due to successive stripping, cleaning, and reassembly. One winter I collected together the older parts and re-assembled the earlier hives.

It is in the plastic parts that most changes are apparent. The earlier frames are a slightly duller orange, have different ridges inside for comb support, and lack the external ridges and writing of the later pattern, save for the much larger APIDEA text on the top bar. They are of course interchangeable down to the point of mixing old and new top bars and side bars. The large ventilation grille has no lip to retain and locate the front of the crownboard, and the feeder queen excluder is of a simpler pattern, more prone to damage or misalignment that might let the queen pass through. Both of these parts, and the queen includer for the entrance, were moulded in a white plastic which yellows with age.

Beyond the detail differences, it's interesting to see how the earlier polystyrene has degraded. Having started out in the same orange/brown (as early marketing photos attest), it has bleached unevenly and lost that orange glow. The exposed polystyrene 'bubbles' have collapsed somewhat, almost in the way that the grain of cedar collapses over time. The newer Apideas which we painted early in their life demonstrate that this has halted such obvious UV degradation of the polystyrene.

What the photo doesn't show is that the earlier polystyrene is roughened and feels easier to abrade. It has shrunk and so all parts move freely to the point of being loose. The roof does not grip, the entrance slider drops down unless supported, and the floor is prone to sliding out if the Apidea is moved around on a surface.

Overall, though, still a perfectly usable mating nuc, even after so many seasons. Buy cheap, buy twice…?

Using Apideas

11.2   Rütli *or* MiniApi

Available from equipment dealer Heinrich Holtermann in Germany, these are precise Apidea copies that feel like an incremental development. All hive body and plastic parts are perfectly interchangeable with the original.

The *Rütli* exudes the same feel of quality, durability, and precision as the original article. It is available in both grey and green polystyrene.

The *MiniApi* is the same design but made in expanded polypropylene, coloured green or brown. It is fully recyclable and claimed to be resistant to UV damage, although knowing how polypropylene degrades I would be sceptical of the long-term durability.

The significant external improvement in both of these copies is that the base of the hive body has square feet at the corners, which fit into corresponding recesses in the corners of the roof. This locates the hives positively when stacked one on top of the other, a feature that the Apidea lacks.

The yellow frames and grilles and such like are all identical to the Apidea equivalents, but this plastic will survive a boil wash. This can make them a useful alternative or source of spares for the original - they are sold separately. Do beware, however, that there are lots of cheap yellow copies of Apidea frames available online, which (just like the original orange ones) do not survive a boil wash. These cheap copies are a bright buttercup yellow compared to the Rütli's pastel yellow parts.

I was very impressed by the Rütli that I ordered. At the time of writing, it retails for €22 compared to €29 for a genuine Apidea. Given that it is all but identical in design and quality, if I were setting up a queen raising enterprise now I would strongly consider the Rütli instead of the Apidea - essentially getting four grey Rütlis for the price of three Apideas.

Using Apideas

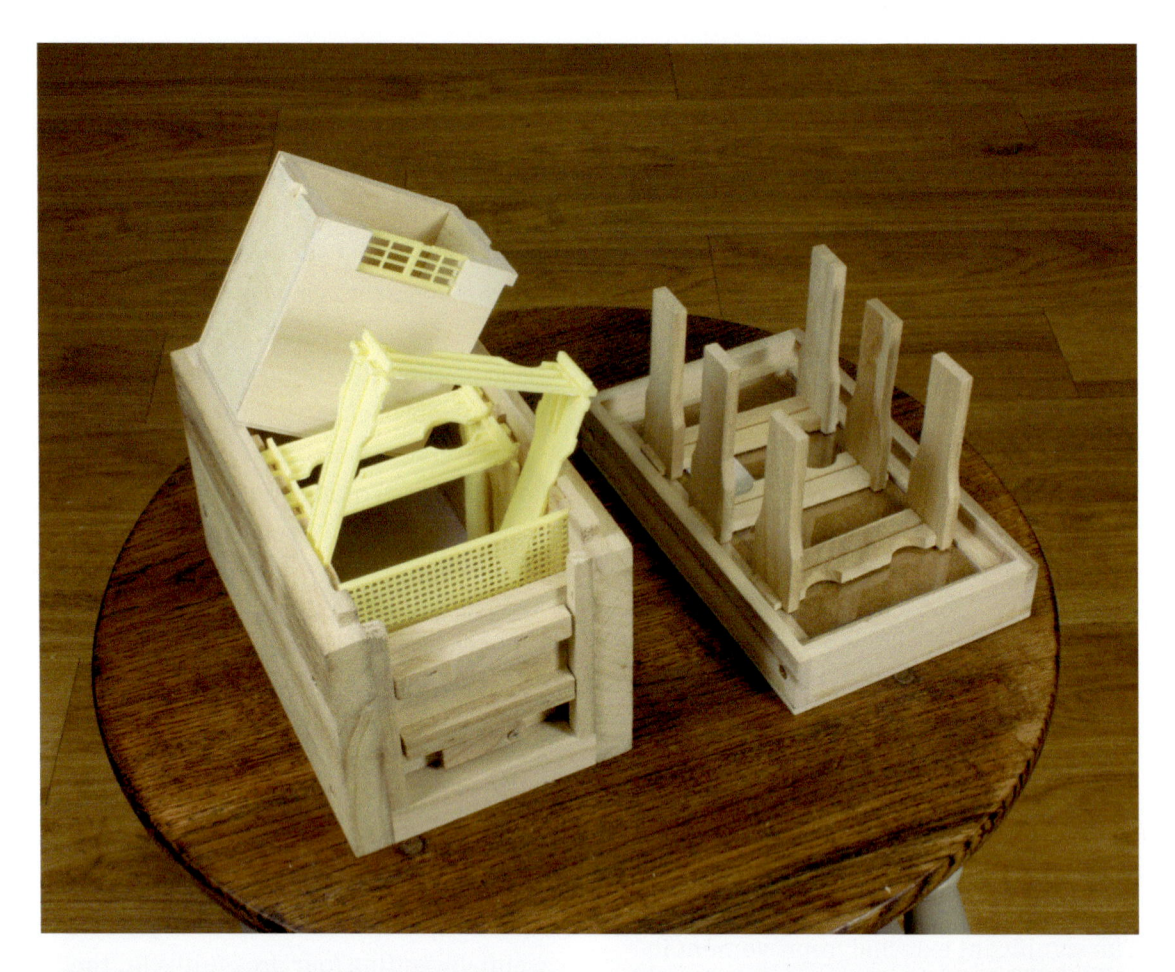

227

11.3 Api'Deus Holz

Right, hold on to your seats for this one. This is a wooden copy of a polystyrene evolution of wooden mating nucs. It loses the additional insulation which was the principal functional differentiator between the polystyrene Apidea and its wooden forbears - and the prime reason that the Apidea was more successful.

I can only assume that this exists due to Germany's particular fervour over the environment. Given that our original poly- and-plastic Apideas are still perfectly usable after forty years, a wooden Apidea does rather appear to be the answer to a question that nobody else was asking.

Even though I am bemused by the rationale, I admire the thought and effort that has gone into making a faithful functioning copy. The texture and grain of wood means that some of the fit and finish is not so precise, and none of the wooden hive parts are interchangeable with their polystyrene or plastic equivalents in the Apidea. However it offers virtually all of the same nice design touches of the original, with the addition of a pivoting wooden entrance slider support that can be moved between fully open, beespace open, and closed. I do wonder how moisture - both from the colony and from the British weather - will affect the fit and movement of the various parts over time?

I found the optional wooden frames to be a little disappointing since they are also sold as a direct replacement for the plastic frames in an Apidea. They are just a fraction too wide across the Hoffman spacers, so they do not sit well together in an Apidea. Whilst a piece of sandpaper and some elbow grease applied to each frame should resolve this, I wouldn't relish doing this for a few hundred frames. However, in the more forgiving tolerances of the wooden hive they do fit and work well.

At the time of writing, the Api'Deus Holz is the same price as an Apidea. It's actually a lovely thing to hold if you are familiar with the Apidea. I have one as a classroom novelty, an interesting talking point during queen raising courses, but will stick to polystyrene mini-nucs for the routine work of queen mating.

Using Apideas

11.4   Swienty Swi-Bine

Danish equipment manufacturer Swienty produce excellent equipment, well engineered and well finished, and cater to both the hobbyist market and to the commercial outfits. Our extracting and bottling rooms are kitted out with mainly Swienty equipment, a decision we have never regretted.

The Swi-Bine is a curious beast. It is clearly a cheaper and simpler version of an Apidea-style mini nuc, and in some respects feels like a squared-off Kieler mating hive as much as it does an Apidea. There are no additional boxes or feeders available. What you see is what you get.

Each design change is just a little less satisfying to use than an Apidea. The crownboard isn't held in place as well, the frames can't be stood upside down without trapping bees, and the plastic sliding floor / filler does not move as well as that of the Apidea. The roof blows off with even the lightest gust of wind, and the whole thing seems to want to fall apart when you turn it over for filling.

The feeder is not removable, just a moulded compartment behind the three frames. This also means the Swi-Bine cannot be expanded from three to five frames. Arguably it is unnecessary for the feeder to be removable, since it is so difficult to to replace without crushing bees - hence the use of feed cartridges. Further, the vast majority of Apideas in use are running perfectly satisfactorily on three frames.

At the time of writing, Swienty list this for €15, alongside to the genuine Apidea at €25, but if you order a significant quantity the Swi-Bine drops to almost half the price of the volume-discounted Apidea.

If you'd never seen an Apidea, I think you'd be content with the Swi-Bine. Similarly, if you need to order a hundred or more mini mating nucs, the cost saving would be significant. However the availability of the Rütli at a price pretty much half way between the Swi-Bine and the Apidea, retaining all the nice design features of the Apidea, means that I would choose the Rütli, even in quantity.

Using Apideas

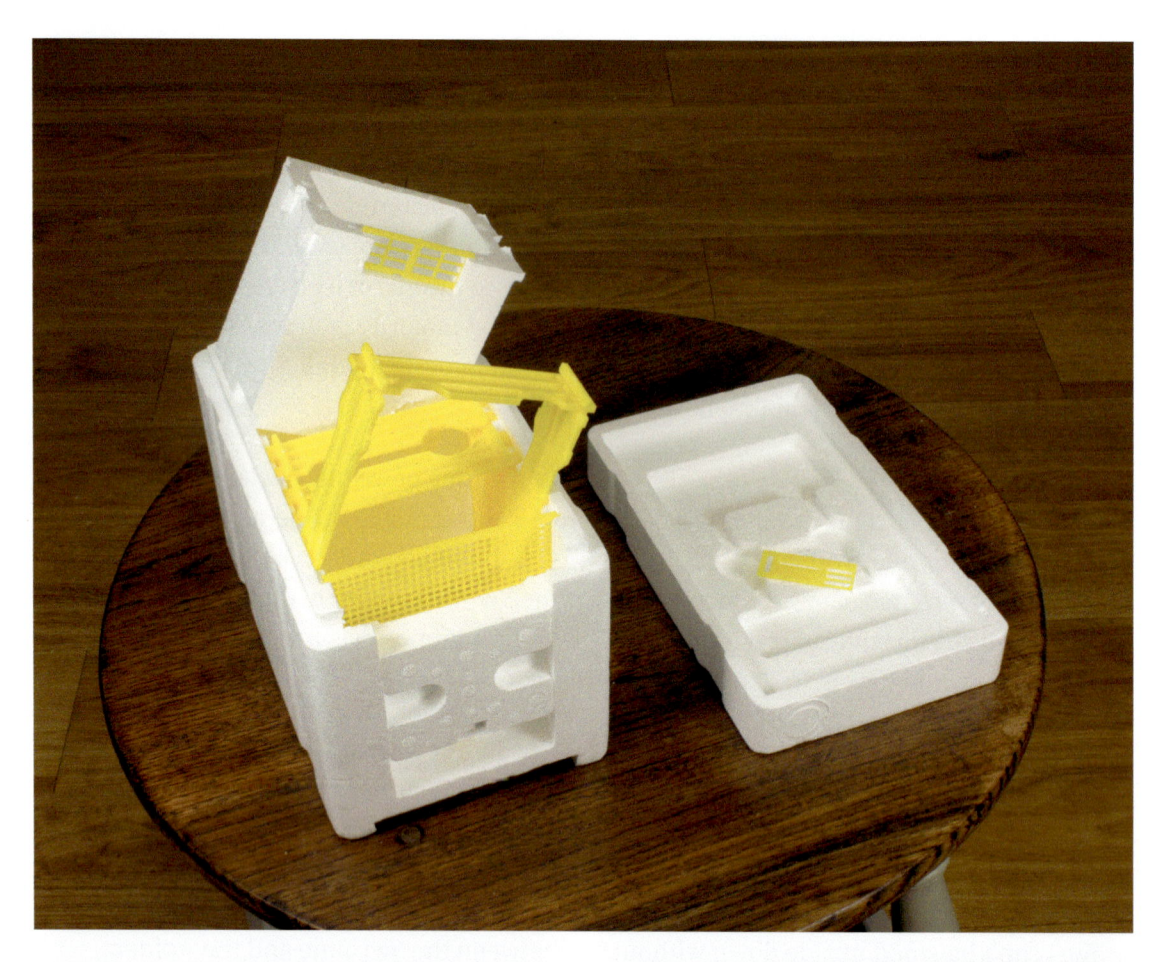

11.5 The white copy

Whilst the outer banding indents on the hive body and roof give the appearance of this being a Swi-Bine copy, the interior dimensions and components are largely direct copies of the Apidea. There are no markings or indication of a brand or manufacturer, although I've noticed that equipment dealers and online sellers often list them with their own (differing!) names.

The feeder compartment, frames, front ventilation grille, and entrance slider are all virtually identical to the Apidea; even a copy of the entrance queen includer is provided. Cut comb container cartridges can be slotted into the feeder, just as in the original. The roof fits snugly and has the same cut-outs in its underside as the Apidea, but there is no crownboard. An introduced queen cells is thus inherently less secure, particularly during establishment when there is no existing comb in the frames into which the cell could be gently pressed.

The major design difference is apparent in the floor arrangement, which appears almost identical to that of the Swi-Bine. A thin piece of plastic slides in and out at the front of the mini-nuc, although two polystyrene 'shelves' (part of the hive body) intrude substantially into the filling aperture. Like the Swi-Bine, the plastic floor has a narrow ventilation grille at the back, which can be exposed to provide additional airflow through the mini-nuc.

In practice, this anonymous white mini-nuc has most of the design of an Apidea, and should therefore work well as a substitute. The polystyrene feels less robust than that of the Apidea - it is easier to compress it and mark it, which indicates that it will be more damage-prone in use.

This white copy currently sells at around two fifths of the price of an Apidea - five white mini-nucs for the price of two brown ones. For some, that would be all that is needed to convince them. For me, this white copy feels flimsy compared to the original, and I have concerns over the durability of that softer polystyrene. I know that Apideas last and last; buy cheap buy twice?

Using Apideas

11.6 The green copy

Another clearly derivative mini-nuc, which shares much in common with the previous anonymous white copy. The inside of the hive body is again largely a direct duplication of the inside of an Apidea, and the frames are the same copies as before. The floor is the same sliding plastic arrangement as with the white one, and the polystyrene similarly feels less robust.

I refer to this as "the green copy" because of the two striking differences, both in green plastic: the disc-type entrance arrangement and the thinner feeder 'bucket'. Interestingly, these two changes allow space for a fourth frame even whilst the feeder is in place. The disc-type entrance is a significant retrograde step, though, since it completely does away with the large red ventilation grille at the front of the Apidea, and hence any real ability to manage ventilation. I would have concerns over this mini-nuc overheating in full sunshine even in British summers.

This time, a clear plastic crownboard is provided, sitting loosely over the top of the box rather than being positively located as in the Apidea. More frustratingly, the hole in the crownboard does not line up with the cut-outs in the frame top bars whichever orientation you try. Worse, though, that hole is a relatively huge 30mm in diameter, meaning that any cell cup that you might use for grafting (Jenter, Cupkit, or JZBZ) is just going to fall straight through with the slightest provocation, leading to failure to emerge.

This green copy provides food for thought. The major change - the entrance - is a distinct step backwards, the crownboard is maddening, and the whole thing just feels naff when compared to a real Apidea. Every change from the original has made it measurably worse to use, adding up to (subtracting down to?) a dismal experience that only just meets a minimum acceptable standard.

This mini-nuc currently sells online at anywhere between 50% - 80% of the cost of an Apidea. You pay substantially more for the additional fiddle and frustration of the green copy over the white copy previously discussed. Remember, even a real Apidea only costs as much as one queen bought in.

Using Apideas

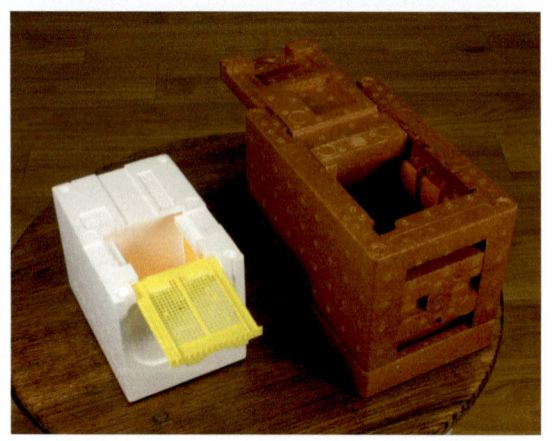

11.7 Mini BiVo

At just 7" long and 5" high, this tiny mini-nuc makes the Apidea look huge.

The polystyrene body and roof are very well moulded and finished, as are the various plastic parts, and there are nice details such as the studs and dimples moulded into the roof and floor respectively to allow multiple mini-nucs to be stacked securely. In short it feels like a high-quality item.

The feeder compartment is fixed, but whilst it is generously proportioned for the size of the Mini BiVo, it is too small to take a cut-comb container feed cartridge. The floor is a ventilated plastic piece which slides open to allow the inverted mini-nuc to be filled with bees. The clear plastic entrance disc offers four choices of aperture: ventilation only, queen includer, fully open, drone includer. There is no crown board.

The two frames are single piece mouldings with an integral plastic 'starter strip' (presumably to be painted with molten wax) and each frame provides 3"x3" of comb area. This gives a total comb area of just 40% of that of an Apidea, suggesting around half a cup of bees would be sufficient to fill the Mini BiVo. Each frame top bar has an arc cut-out for the introduction of a queen cell. Testing with the various cell cups, Jenter and Cupkit 'corks' need the frames aligned for D-shaped opening, although neither arrangement gives the same degree of security as such a cell cup cork suspended through the crownboard of an Apidea. JZBZs need the support of card squares with either frame orientation. The frame topbars have moulded tabs which serve no obvious purpose yet prevent frames from being stood inverted and upright whilst removed during an inspection.

I haven't yet run one of these to see how it compares. On the one hand, the quality and small size make it appealing, on the other hand the small population suggests it would be more vulnerable in changeable weather. This latter risk is mitigated by the relatively large feeder compartment which holds a generous amount of fondant for such a small colony. I also don't like the lack of security for an inserted queen cell

At the time of writing, these are retailing for around two thirds of the price of an Apidea. I'd love to hear the experiences of somebody who has run these in quantity for a number of seasons.

237

12 Resources

In this chapter I present a number of printed items that I have developed to assist in the managing of Apideas. All are available to download from the Advanced Beekeeping Courses website at

www.advancedbeekeeping.org.uk/resources.

Using Apideas

12.1 Simple grafting calculator

Counting backwards or forwards ten days sounds simple, but can be surprisingly error-prone, particularly when crossing the end of one month and the start of the next. I created a simple sliding calculator to allow me to verify my date calculations.

This allows me to work both ways between the graft and move on days. The example below is showing that if I graft on Saturday of this week, I need to be ready to move on the resulting ripe queen cells on Tuesday of the week after next.

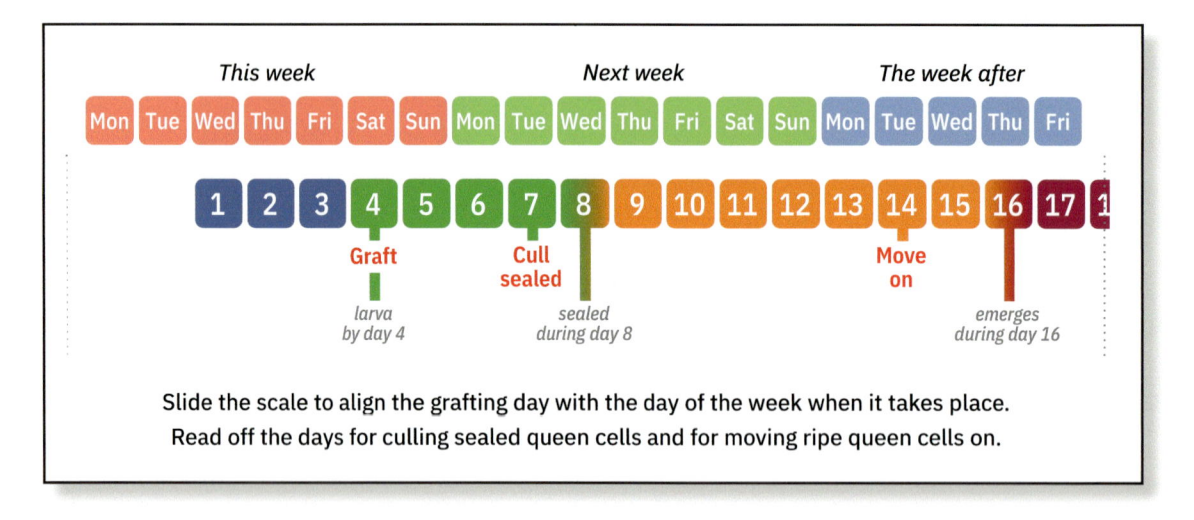

Instructions are given on the sheet for how to cut out the sliding section and to slit below the scale to fit this in. This is best printed on medium or heavy weight card - check what your printer is capable of handling.

12.2 In/out cards

Taking Apideas out after three days in the dark sounds straightforward until you forget when you put them in the dark. The in/out cards aim to make this foolproof - by having the corresponding 'in' and 'out' days printed on each side.

When you put the Apideas in the dark, find today's **in** card, flip it over so that it shows the corresponding **out** day, and place it on top of those Apideas.

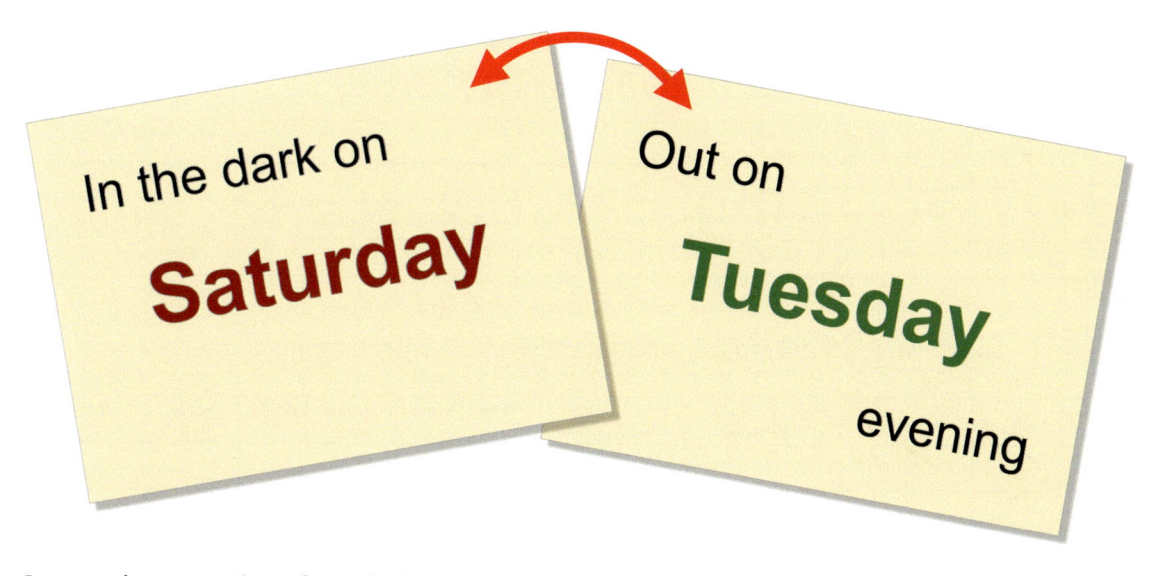

Instructions are given for printing using either a single-sided printer or a duplex printer. For extra durability, laminate the resulting printed cards using a simple document laminator and A6 laminating pouches.

12.3 Apidea inspection record sheets

In **Chapter 3** *Establishment* I mentioned that I had tried a number of different record sheets for recording the subset of hive inspection information that is appropriate when using Apideas. I have concluded that there is no single perfect record sheet, so have given you two examples to try out. Three beekeepers, four opinions, indeed! Remember that for each of these sheets, the intention is that you start a new line of records for an Apidea when it is first established, and then each time it is recycled.

Version 2 sheet - status check boxes with notes for up to six inspections: Overwrite the 'date' headings with the inspection date, record notes for that inspection in that column..

No.	QC date	QE	Eggs	Brood	Clip + mark	date	date	date	date	date	date

Version 4 sheet - status & date focus, without individual inspection notes:

Apidea no.	QC date	QE ?	VQS ?	Eggs ?	Eggs date	Marked ?	Mark date	Q no.	Brood ?	Brood date	Ready ?	Ready date	Notes

Whilst v4 is much more explicit about what has happened and when, my preference is for v2: it is simpler, and I still like to be able to note tasks and any incidental observations at each inspection. Generally six inspections are enough for each queen cell cycle.

The PDF and XLS files of both of these record sheets give some suggested abbreviations e.g. QC = queen cell, QE = queen emerged, VQS = virgin queen seen.

Laser print onto water-resistant paper, and write with either a pencil or a waterproof biro. *Rite in the Rain* paper is excellent; a *Tombow Airpress* pressurised ballpoint pen is chunky but very effective, and costs just £7 at the time of writing. Use both with a plastic clipboard - tie the pen on with a good length of string or it will get lost in the grass!

Resources

12.3.1 Using the record sheets

With either of the example record sheets, one single line represents one cycle of queen mating per mini-nuc. Once a mating cycle has either succeeded or failed, the mini-nuc will be recycled, re-established, or closed down. At this point the current record line is scored out; when a mini-nuc is recycled or re-established, a new record line is started.

With the v2 sheet, the 'date' columns can get jumbled, and you may run out of them, unless you start new records on a new sheet for every concurrent group of established or recycled mini-nucs. This allows you to start recording the inspections for that group of mini-nucs in the left-most 'date' column of their sheet (rather than starting half-way across and then running out of columns for later inspections).Potentially you may be starting a new sheet at any visit to the mating apiary, however this will make record-keeping easier in the long run.

Here is an example of the v2 record sheets in use over successive inspections:

No.	QC date	QE	Eggs	Brood	Clip + mark	9/5 date	date	date	date	date	date
7	4/5	✓				QE					
13	4/5	✓				QE					
~~15~~	~~4/5~~	✗				~~QNE~~					

No.	QC date	QE	Eggs	Brood	Clip + mark	9/5 date	14/5 date	date	date	date	date
7	4/5	✓				QE	VQS				
13	4/5	✓				QE	VQS				
~~15~~	~~4/5~~	✗				~~QNE~~					

No.	QC date	QE	Eggs	Brood	Clip + mark	9/5 date	14/5 date	23/5 date	29/5 date	date	date
7	4/5	✓				QE	VQS	VQS weak			
13	4/5	✓	✓		✓	QE	VQS	C+M			
~~15~~	~~4/5~~	✗				~~QNE~~					

242

Using Apideas

12.4 Establishment checklists

The checklists shown on the clipboard illustrations in **Chapter 3** *Establishment* can be downloaded to print and use. You may find these useful in physically ticking off equipment and steps required for establishment, particularly when doing this for the first time.

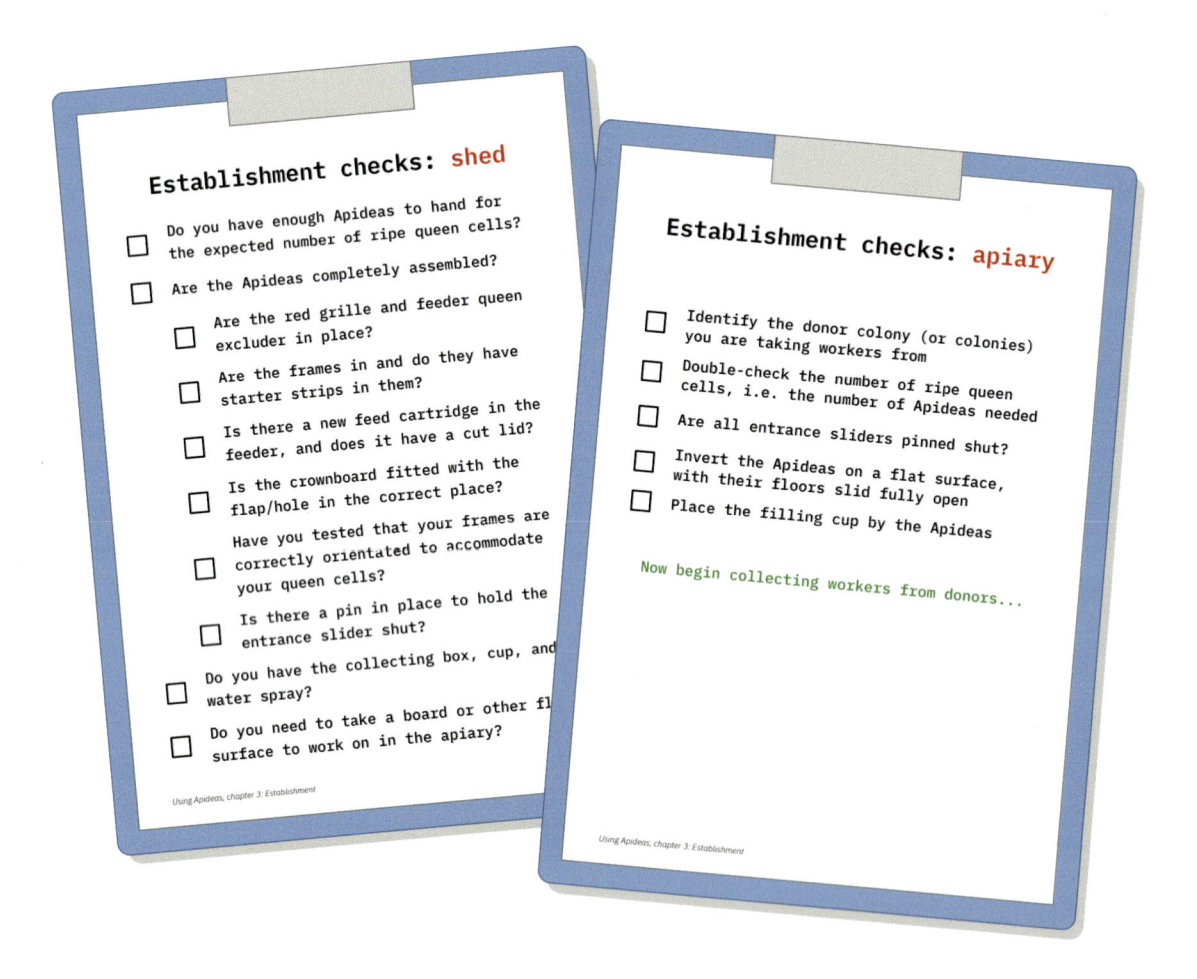

Establishment checks: shed
- ☐ Do you have enough Apideas to hand for the expected number of ripe queen cells?
- ☐ Are the Apideas completely assembled?
  - ☐ Are the red grille and feeder queen excluder in place?
  - ☐ Are the frames in and do they have starter strips in them?
  - ☐ Is there a new feed cartridge in the feeder, and does it have a cut lid?
  - ☐ Is the crownboard fitted with the flap/hole in the correct place?
  - ☐ Have you tested that your frames are correctly orientated to accommodate your queen cells?
  - ☐ Is there a pin in place to hold the entrance slider shut?
- ☐ Do you have the collecting box, cup, and water spray?
- ☐ Do you need to take a board or other fl[at] surface to work on in the apiary?

Using Apideas, chapter 3: Establishment

Establishment checks: apiary
- ☐ Identify the donor colony (or colonies) you are taking workers from
- ☐ Double-check the number of ripe queen cells, i.e. the number of Apideas needed
- ☐ Are all entrance sliders pinned shut?
- ☐ Invert the Apideas on a flat surface, with their floors slid fully open
- ☐ Place the filling cup by the Apideas

Now begin collecting workers from donors...

Using Apideas, chapter 3: Establishment

243

Resources

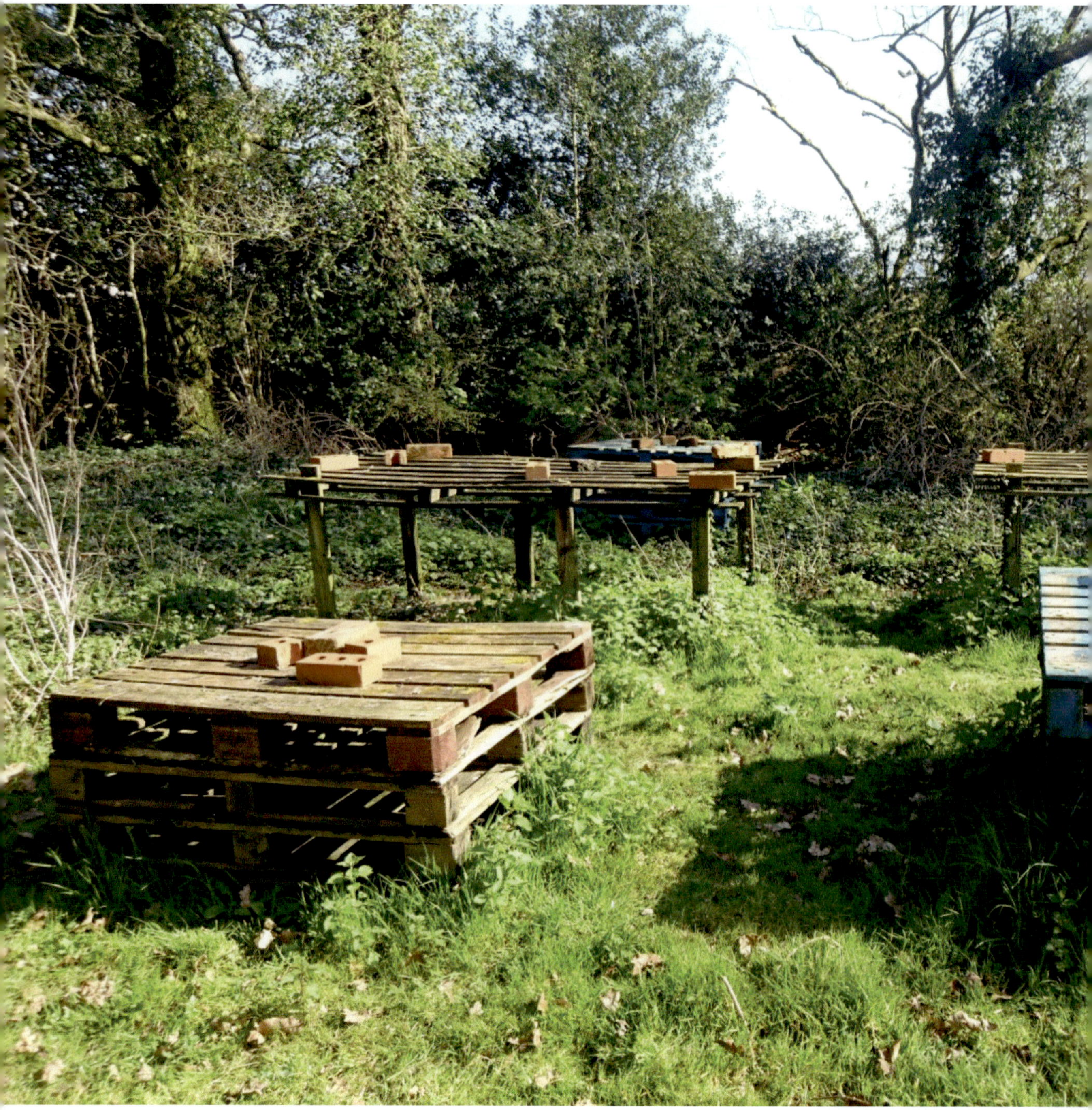

13 Closing thoughts

It's October as I'm finishing this book. The Apideas have long since been united onto colonies, and their tables lie empty in the mating apiary. All the pleasure of working with these little colonies is now over for this year. There will be plenty of time during the coming months to reflect on what went well, and what could be done better or differently next year.

It has been quite a journey documenting and photographing our experiences and techniques. We've had some great discussions, my father and I, recalling the successes and the failures of seasons past. There's been plenty of "Why did we start doing this?" and "Why did we stop doing that?", and it's really challenged us to review the rationale for so much that has become our habitual practice.

I said in the introduction that much of my fondness for Apideas comes from my enjoyment of queen raising. Actually, the reciprocal is true: much of my fondness for queen raising comes from the enjoyment of using Apideas. They really are so well designed for their intended purpose. I haven't really tried to conceal my feeling that the original is best (with one notable exception) and that the true value of some pieces of equipment is only realised after many years of successful use.

If you like our approach and perspective, why not consider joining us on our courses at our honey farm? We have some of the best facilities in the country for training, we concentrate on practical hands-on development for experienced beekeepers, and our honey farm is located just three miles from the coast in a lovely unspoilt part of the country. Course dates and details are listed on our website

www.advancedbeekeeping.org.uk

Above all, thank you for coming on this journey with me. I hope that you have found plenty to consider, and plenty to inspire you. Enjoy your beekeeping!

Dan Basterfield
Blackbury Honey Farm, October 2022

61
8
7
36
38
45
41
47
33
52
91
11
50
12
87
69
4
5
94
28
83
25
20
40
96
49
55
9
80
43
82
34
17
86
22

Index

Absconding 16
Advanced Beekeeping Courses 8
Ambrosia 193
Apidea
    5 frame 166
    8 frame and 10 frame 171
    adaptor frames 176–177, 181
    assembly 25
    carrying 45
    copies 222
    early pattern 224
    in vehicles 46
    original 5
    over-wintering 182
    revert to 3 frames 170
    shade 37, 150, 186
    sterilising 162, 207, 210–211
    upper brood box 130, 171, 181
Badgers 47, 197–198
Balancing populations 127
    adult bees 129, 189
    brood transfer 124, 127, 152, 179, 181, 189
    emerging brood 130
    exchange 128
Bee space 29
Black Queen Cell Virus (BQCV) 148
Bleach 207, 211
Broodless 124
Broodright 124–125
Chalkbrood 162, 191

Checklist 68–69, 243
Chronic Bee Paralysis Virus (CBPV) 160
Cleaning 162, 183, 206–208
    process 207–208
    tools 209
Closing down 119, 132
Cohesion 15, 23, 84, 87, 123–125, 146, 160
    brood pheromone 124–125, 180
    queenright & broodright 124
Colour of emerging brood 130
Comb
    bracing 90
    drawing 23, 31–32, 178–179
Condensation 173
Crownboard 28, 41
    flap 115–116
    flex 101
    hole 32–35
    yellowing 214
Cupkit 32–33, 46
Cut comb container 40
    cut lid 41
Deformed Wing Virus (DWV) 160, 190
Disease
    chalkbrood 191
    dealing with 189
    dysentery 191–192
    nosema 191
    varroa 190
Double brood box 171–173, 181
Drones 72, 79, 103, 110, 126, 175, 190

Using Apideas

drone brood 179–180
drone includers 175
drone starter strips 180
Duct tape 214
Dusk 87
Eggs
    checking for 96
    laying 103, 154
    multiple eggs 154, 156, 158
Entrance activity 150
Entrance slider 36
    introduction cages 115–116
    pin to secure 36, 63, 115, 186
    queen includer 175
    slack vs stiff 36
    ventilation 36–37, 84, 116, 182, 186
Establishment phase 12, 35
    cast swarm analogy 66, 179
    filling with bees 39, 71
    number of bees 55
    preparation 68
    principle 66
    process 66–67, 77
    putting out 24, 87
    storing in the dark 23, 84
    two chances 89
Fanning 88, 150
Feeder 39–40
    cartridge 40, 43, 51, 100–102
    checking 100, 102, 164, 183
    hefting 102
    queen excluder 28
    queen trapped in 156
    removable 41, 96, 101, 166
    replacing 100
    roof feeder 169, 182–183
    sugar syrup 39, 174
    top feeder 39, 174

    workers clustering in 23, 89, 146
Feeding 100, 174
Filling cup
    making 54–55
    using 75–76
Filling with bees 71
    collecting box 71, 75
    cup or scoop 75–76
    distribution 75, 77
    donor colony 72–73, 78, 80, 117, 188, 190
    drawn comb 178
    drones 72, 79
    process 72, 74, 77
    selective collection 79–80
    start again 79
    throwing bees 76–78
    too few bees 78
    turning Apideas 78–79
    water spray 73, 86
Flight path 49
Fondant 22, 40–42, 100, 169, 174
    cake icing 44
    cutting 42
    dry 40
    ingredients 43
    introduction cages 110
    moist 43
    recovered 100
    slumping 40
Foundation 167
    coloured 31–32
    cutting starter strips 30
    not drawn 146, 148
Frame
    assembly 26–27, 29
    boiling 210
    broken 212
    castellated runners 97

Index

checking 95, 182
cleaning 209–210
dimensions 176
foundation 27
Hoffman spacing 97, 177
incorrect assembly 27
orientation 32, 34–35
propolised 97–98, 177, 183
removing to inspect 95
spare frames 29
starter strip 30–31, 180, 210
Gloves 106
Grafting calculator 239
Health status 188–189
Heinrich Holtermann 175, 219, 226
Herding cats 39, 96
Hive tool 52, 97
J-tool 52–53, 97–98
mini tools 53
Taylor's Eye Witness 52–53
Honey stores 152, 167, 181
Hornets 193, 195
Hygiene 188
IKEA 216
In/Out cards 85–86, 240
Inspecting Apideas 94
checking frames 95–96, 142
damage 97
double brood 172–173
frames 94, 99
methodical 94
propolised frames 97–98, 183
unpacking 94
upturned roof 94, 107
Inspection timing 92
Introduction cages 110–111
aggression 134
attendants 110, 113–114
caging queen and workers 111–112
familiarisation 117
fondant 110
guillotining 113
holding in Apideas 115
numbering 110, 117
queenlessness test 117–118
re-introduction 117–118
Jenter 21, 32–33, 46
original system 33
JZBZ 32, 34, 46
card holders 34
Lego brick 37
Management phase 12, 92
Masonry paint 216–217
Mice 199–200
Mini BiVo 236
MiniApi 226
Misconceptions
foundation orientation 152
handling queens 106
Requirement for shade 37, 186
Saving a laying worker colony 158
workers with caged queen 113
National Diploma in Beekeeping 7
Navigation 216
Nosema 191
Nucleus colonies 114
Numbering
all four sides 60
allocation sheet 61
duplicates 61
fading 61
label stickers 61
marker pen 60
Observation hive 32

250

Out apiary 68, 71, 97, 175
Overcrowding 150, 152, 166
    during unite 138
Overheating 37, 84, 186
Overwintering 132, 182, 203
Painting 60, 206, 216
    brushes 216
    coverage 216
    dyes and pigments 216–217
    harlequin hives 218
    masonry paint 217
Petrol 189
Polystyrene
    damage 97, 213–214, 220
Poor weather 100, 102, 116, 154, 164, 169, 172
Population size 89, 144, 146
Propolis 37, 207
Push pin 36
    colour system 62, 125
    compartmental box 63
    entrance slider 63
    pinholes 37
Queen
    attractiveness 23
    balling 92, 113, 150
    biting of 15, 160
    clipping and marking 103, 106
    damaged 113, 160
    development times 17, 93, 125
    developmental changes 18
    drone layer 154
    egg laying 21, 95, 103, 154, 156
    finding 96
    grabbers 107
    holding after mating 15, 132, 166, 171, 175, 182
    immobilising 103–104
    introduction 113, 134
    introduction by uniting 119
    lost 113, 218
    mating 20
    mating flight 88, 92, 96, 128, 150
    mating variability 126
    picking 103–108, 111–112
    racial differences 114
    re-introduction 117–118
    regicide 190
    steering 103
    virgin 96, 103, 107, 142
Queen cell
    adding 23, 81, 84, 169, 172
    caging 21–22
    candling 82–83
    destroyed 17
    dropped 26, 34, 46, 81
    emergence 18, 22–23, 87, 89
    emergency 23, 125–126, 152
    failure to emerge 34, 81, 88–89, 146, 148
    frame gap 81
    gentle shaking 83
    heel of wax 35
    moving day 19–22
    natural 34–35
    prompt removal 90
    protector 35
    ripe 2, 18–19, 24, 81, 89, 124, 126
    thinned tip 22
    viable and non-viable 23
Queen includer 28, 175
Queen raising
    Alley strip 35
    batches 16
    capacity 16, 175
    grafting 33
    inherent losses 16

Miller method 35
outcomes 126
pipeline 15, 123–124, 175
records 19, 21
safety margin 19
scheduling 17, 19, 22
timescale 17
Queenless 23, 88, 117, 119, 123–125, 132, 190
implications 124–125
testing for 117–118
Queenright 124
Reading bees 142
Record sheets 52, 58–59, 96, 241–242
Records simplified 56
Recycling phase 15, 122
decision 119
Red grille 27, 37, 85, 115, 182, 186
cleaning 210
propolis 186
repairs 215
Repairs 212
crownboard 214
frames 212
polystyrene 213–214
red grille 215
Rite in the Rain 241
Robbing 39
Roof
alignment 25, 81
cut-outs 25, 33, 81, 115
replacing 82
sweeping movement 82
upside down 95, 172–173
weights 87
Rütli 226
Sealed stores 39
Shaking out 125, 162

Smoke 101, 117, 173
Soapy water 85
Spare parts 219
Staged introduction 114, 132, 134
Stands and tables 47, 87
Apidea arrangement 49, 88, 94
bench 47
height 47
improvised 88
pallet 48–49
pallets, jumbo 50
post stands 47
straps 50
weights 50, 87
Starvation 132, 164, 182
revival 164
Stickiness 102
Stone markers 62
Storage 199, 201, 206, 211, 220
Storing in the dark 84
in/out cards 85–86
overheating 84
spraying water 84–85
Swarm
cast swarm 12, 66, 87, 179
Swienty 79, 110
puzzle cage 110
Swi-Bine 79, 230
Temperature 184
monitoring 184–186
Three feet or three miles 87
Tombow Airpress 241
Toolkit 51
Transporting Apideas 97
Uniting 119, 132–133, 135, 137–139, 182
follow up 135, 138
newspaper 133, 135–137, 139

252

    queen excluder 136, 138
    staged 134
    to nucleus 133–134, 136, 139

UV damage 206, 216

Varroa 160, 181, 190
    out of sequence treatment 190

Vaso Trap lids 192

Ventilation 84, 116, 167, 182, 186

Wallpaper scraper 42

Washing machine 210

Washing soda 207, 209

Wasps 192
    baits 193–195
    by-catch 196
    decoy trapping 195
    period of threat 192
    traps 192–196

Water spray 72–73, 84, 86, 129

Wax moth 201–202, 214, 220

Wet weather 93

Wood filler 213

Woodpeckers 203–204

Worker bees
    aggression to queen 160, 190
    attendants 110, 113–114, 133, 169, 172
    clustering in feeder 23, 148
    crushing 107, 109, 170, 173, 178
    dispersal 24, 89, 125, 146, 162, 189, 191
    fanning 150
    interest in caged queen 117
        aggressively 118, 134
    laying workers 124–125, 156, 158
    picking 111–113
    retention 24, 128

Working space 49, 71